everyday Comprehens

MW00444043

Intervention Activities

Table of Contents

Using Everyday Comprehension Intervention Activities ii

Unit 1: Making Predictions in Fiction 1

Unit 2: Making Predictions in Nonfiction. 7

Unit 3: Identifying Sequence of Events in Fiction 13

Unit 4: Identifying Sequence of Events in Nonfiction. 19

Unit 5: Analyzing Story Elements: Setting 25

Unit 6: Analyzing Story Elements: Plot 31

Unit 7: Analyzing Character: Traits and Feelings 37

Unit 8: Analyzing Character: Relationships and Changes 43

Unit 9: Identifying Stated Main Idea and Supporting Details 49

Unit 10: Identifying Unstated Main Idea and Supporting Details 55

Unit 11: Summarizing Fiction. 61

Unit 12: Summarizing Nonfiction 67

Unit 13: Comparing and Contrasting in Fiction 73

Unit 14: Comparing and Contrasting in Nonfiction. 79

Unit 15: Identifying Cause and Effect in Fiction 85

Unit 16: Identifying Cause and Effect in Nonfiction. 91

Unit 17: Making Inferences in Fiction 97

Unit 18: Making Inferences in Nonfiction. 103

Unit 19: Drawing Conclusions in Fiction 109

Unit 20: Drawing Conclusions in Nonfiction. 115

Unit 21: Evaluating Author's Purpose in Fiction. 121

Unit 22: Evaluating Author's Purpose in Nonfiction 127

Unit 23: Analyzing Text Structure and Organization in Fiction 133

Unit 24: Analyzing Text Structure and Organization in Nonfiction. . . . 139

Unit 25: Using Text Features to Locate Information 145

Unit 26: Using Graphic Features to Interpret Information 151

Unit 27: Distinguishing and Evaluating Fact and Opinion I 157

Unit 28: Distinguishing and Evaluating Fact and Opinion II. 163

Unit 29: Making Judgments I 169

Unit 30: Making Judgments II 175

Why Use Everyday Comprehension Intervention Activities?

Reading with full text comprehension is the ultimate goal of all reading instruction. Students who read the words but don't comprehend them aren't really reading at all. Research has shown that explicit comprehension strategy instruction helps students understand and remember what they read, which allows them to communicate what they've learned with others and perform better in testing situations.

Although some students master comprehension strategies easily during regular classroom instruction, many others need additional re-teaching opportunities to master these essential strategies. The Everyday Intervention Activities series provides easy-to-use, five-day intervention units for Grades K–5. These units are structured around a research- based Model-Guide-Practice-Apply approach. You can use these activities in a variety of intervention models, including Response to Intervention (RTI).

Getting Started

In just five simple steps, Everyday Comprehension Intervention Activities provides everything you need to identify students' comprehension needs and to provide targeted, research-based intervention.

1. PRE-ASSESS to identify students' comprehension needs.

Use the pre-assessment to identify the strategies your students need to master.

2. MODEL the strategy.

Every five-day unit targets a specific strategy. On Day 1, use the teacher prompts and reproducible activity to introduce and model the strategy.

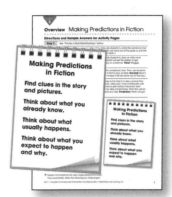

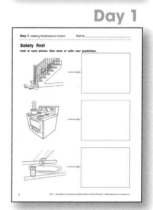

Day 1

3. GUIDE PRACTICE and APPLY.

Use the reproducible practice activities for Days 2, 3, and 4 to build students' understanding of, and proficiency with, the strategy.

Day 2 **Day 3** **Day 4**

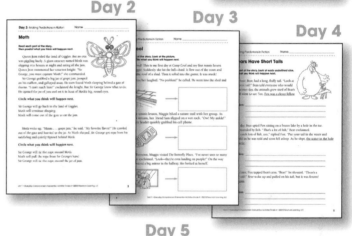

Day 5

4. MONITOR progress.

Administer the Day 5 reproducible assessment to monitor each student's progress and to make instructional decisions.

5. POST-ASSESS to document student progress.

Use the post-assessment to measure students' progress as a result of your interventions.

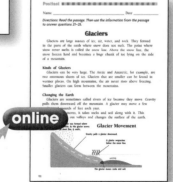

Standards-Based Comprehension Strategies in Everyday Intervention Activities

The comprehension strategies found in the Everyday Intervention Activities series are introduced developmentally and spiral from one grade to the next based on curriculum standards across a variety of states. The chart below shows the comprehension strategies addressed at each grade level in this series.

Comprehension Strategy	Strategy Definition	K	1	2	3	4	5
Make Predictions	Determine what might happen next in a story or nonfiction piece. Predictions are based on information presented in the text.	✔	✔	✔	✔	✔	✔
Identify Sequence of Events	Determine the order of events for topics such as history, science, or biography. Determine the steps to make or do something.	✔	✔	✔	✔	✔	✔
Analyze Story Elements	Analyze the setting and plot (problem/solution) in a fiction text.	✔	✔	✔	✔	✔	✔
Analyze Character	Analyze story characters based on information and on clues and evidence in the text, including description, actions, dialogue, feelings, and traits.	✔	✔	✔	✔	✔	✔
Identify Main Idea and Supporting Details	Determine what the paragraph, page, or chapter is mostly about. Sometimes the main idea is stated and sometimes it is implied. Students must choose details that support the main idea, not "just any detail."	✔	✔	✔	✔	✔	✔
Summarize	Take key ideas from the text and put them together to create a shorter version of the original text. Summaries should have few, if any, details.	✔	✔	✔	✔	✔	✔
Compare and Contrast	Find ways that two things are alike and different.	✔	✔	✔	✔	✔	✔
Identify Cause and Effect	Find things that happened (effect) and why they happened (cause). Text may contain multiple causes and effects.	✔	✔	✔	✔	✔	✔
Make Inferences	Determine what the author is suggesting without directly stating it. Inferences are usually made during reading and are made from one or two pieces of information from the text. Students' inferences will vary but must be made from the evidence in the text and background knowledge.	✔	✔	✔	✔	✔	✔
Draw Conclusions	Determine what the author is suggesting without directly stating it. Conclusions are made during and after reading, and are made from multiple (3+) pieces of information from the text. Students' conclusions will vary but must be drawn from the evidence in the text and background knowledge.		✔	✔	✔	✔	✔
Evaluate Author's Purpose	Determine why the author wrote the passage or used certain information. A book can have more than one purpose. Purposes include to entertain, to inform, and to persuade.				✔	✔	✔
Analyze Text Structure and Organization	Determine the text structure to better understand what the author is saying and to use as research when text must be analyzed.				✔	✔	✔
Use Text Features to Locate Information	Use text features (bullets, captions, glossary, index, sidebars) to enhance meaning.				✔	✔	✔
Use Graphic Features to Interpret Information	Use clues from graphic features (charts, maps, graphs) to determine what is not stated in the text or to enhance meaning.				✔	✔	✔
Distinguish and Evaluate Facts and Opinions	Recognize objective statements of fact and subjective opinions within a nonfiction text.					✔	✔
Make Judgments	Use facts from the text and prior knowledge and beliefs to make and confirm opinions about the characters or situations.					✔	✔

Everyday Comprehension Intervention Activities Grade 4 • © 2010 Newmark Learning, LLC

Using Everyday Intervention for RTI

According to the National Center on Response to Intervention, RTI "integrates assessment and intervention within a multi-level prevention system to maximize student achievement and to reduce behavior problems." This model of instruction and assessment allows schools to identify at-risk students, monitor their progress, provide research-proven interventions, and "adjust the intensity and nature of those interventions depending on a student's responsiveness."

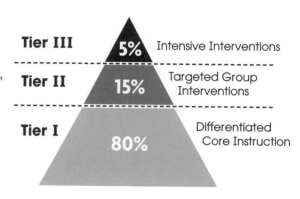

RTI models vary from district to district, but the most prevalent model is a three-tiered approach to instruction and assessment.

The Three Tiers of RTI	Using Everyday Intervention Activities
Tier I: Differentiated Core Instruction • Designed for all students • Preventive, proactive, standards-aligned instruction • Whole- and small-group differentiated instruction • Ninety-minute, daily core reading instruction in the five essential skill areas: phonics, phonemic awareness, comprehension, vocabulary, fluency	• Use whole-group comprehension mini-lessons to introduce and guide practice with comprehension strategies that all students need to learn. • Use any or all of the units in the order that supports your core instructional program.
Tier II: Targeted Group Interventions • For at-risk students • Provide thirty minutes of daily instruction beyond the ninety-minute Tier I core reading instruction • Instruction is conducted in small groups of three to five students with similar needs	• Select units based on your students' areas of need (the pre-assessment can help you identify these). • Use the units as week-long, small-group mini-lessons.
Tier III: Intensive Interventions • For high-risk students experiencing considerable difficulty in reading • Provide up to sixty minutes of additional intensive intervention each day in addition to the ninety-minute Tier I core reading instruction • More intense and explicit instruction • Instruction conducted individually or with smaller groups of one to three students with similar needs	• Select units based on your students' areas of need. • Use the units as one component of an intensive comprehension intervention program.

Overview Making Predictions in Fiction

Directions and Sample Answers for Activity Pages

Day 1	See "Provide a Real-World Example" below.
Day 2	Read and discuss each part of the story. Then ask students to circle the sentence that tells what they think will happen next. (**First:** Moth will come out of the gate to eat the jam. **Second:** Sir George will tie the rope around Moth.)
Day 3	Read and discuss each part of the story. Then ask students to draw or write what they think will happen next. (**First:** The tennis teacher will use the ladder to get the ball. **Second:** Two adults will carry Sam away on a stretcher. **Third:** Maggie will see a butterfly on her head.)
Day 4	Read each part of the story together. Discuss the underlined clues. Then ask students to write their predictions. (**First:** Fox will think of a trick to play on Bear. **Second:** Bear's tail will get stuck in ice. **Third:** Only a small part of Bear's tail will come out of the ice.)
Day 5	Read the story together. Ask students to use clues in the story to make a prediction and record their ideas on their graphic organizers. Afterward, meet individually with students to discuss their results. Use their responses to plan further instruction and review. (**Clues:** Molly will watch the show until her dad comes home. Then she will do her homework. Her dad will be there if she needs any help. **Prediction:** Molly will get a good grade on the math test.)

Provide a Real-World Example

◆ Hand out the Day 1 activity page.

◆ **Say:** *Sometimes accidents happen in a home. These accidents often happen because of unsafe conditions. We can often predict, or make a good guess, that an accident might happen and use this information to prevent the accident.*

◆ Ask students to look at the first picture. **Ask:** *What clues do you see that an accident might happen? What do you already know about these clues? What do you predict might happen?*

◆ Allow time for students to draw or write their predictions in the blank box and share them with the group. Repeat the process with the steaming pot left on the stove and the drinking glass beside the bathroom sink.

◆ Invite students to share their predictions. **Ask:** *What clues did you use? What do you already know that helped you make your prediction?* Discuss what people could do to make each situation safer.

◆ Explain that students can also make predictions when they read stories. Write the following on chart paper:

**Making Predictions
in Fiction**

**Find clues in the story
and pictures.**

**Think about what you
already know.**

**Think about what
usually happens.**

**Think about what you
expect to happen
and why.**

Safety First

Look at each picture. Then draw or write your predictions.

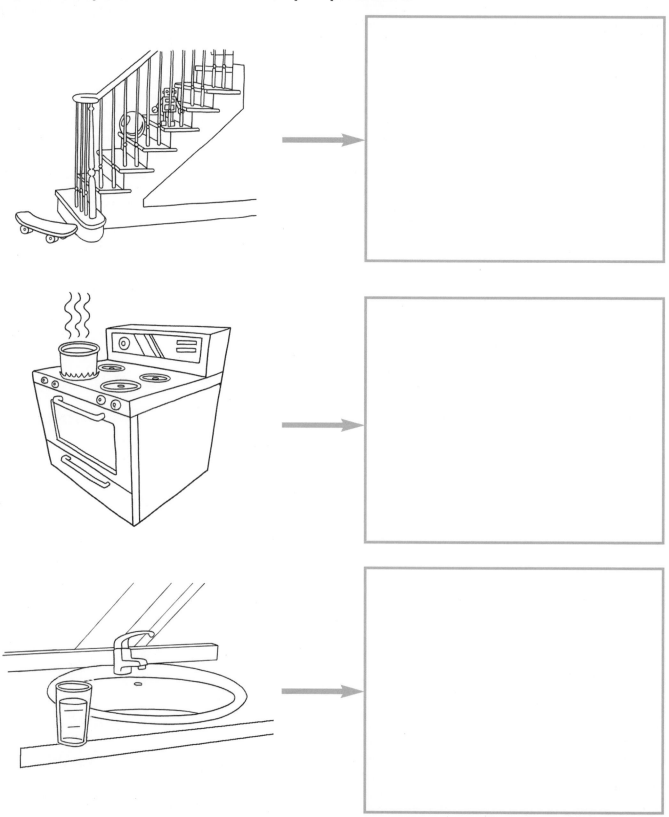

Moth

Read each part of the story.
Then predict what you think will happen next.

Queen Jean ruled the land of Giggles. But no one was giggling lately. A giant creature named Moth was slipping into houses at night and eating all the jam. Queen Jean summoned her smartest knight. "Sir George, you must capture Moth!" she commanded.

Sir George grabbed a big jar of grape jam, jumped on his stallion, and galloped away. He soon found Moth sleeping behind a gate of thorns. "I can't reach him!" exclaimed the knight. But Sir George knew what to do. He opened the jar of jam and set it in front of Moth's big, round eyes.

Circle what you think will happen next.

Sir George will go back to the land of Giggles.
Moth will continue sleeping.
Moth will come out of the gate to eat the jam.

Moth woke up. "Mmm . . . grape jam," he said. "My favorite flavor!" He crawled out of the gate and hurried to the jar. As Moth slurped, Sir George got rope from his saddlebag and quietly tiptoed behind Moth.

Circle what you think will happen next.

Sir George will tie the rope around Moth.
Moth will pull the rope from Sir George's hand.
Sir George will tie the rope around the jar of jam.

Camp Cool

Read each part of the story. Look at the picture.
Then draw or write what you think will happen next.

"I'm so excited! This is my first day at Camp Cool and my first tennis lesson ever," said Maggie. Suddenly, she hit the ball—hard. It flew out of the court and bounced onto the roof of a shed. Then it rolled into the gutter. It was stuck!

The tennis teacher laughed. "No problem!" he called. He went into the shed and got a ladder.

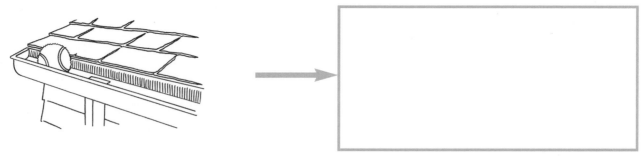

After her tennis lesson, Maggie hiked a nature trail with her group. As they crossed a stream, her friend Sam slipped on a wet rock. "Ow! My ankle!" he called. Their leader quickly grabbed his cell phone.

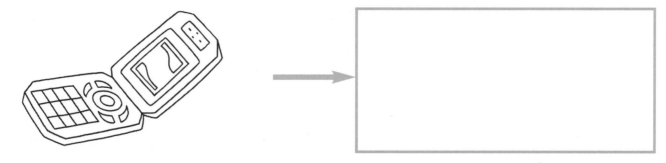

Later that afternoon, Maggie visited The Butterfly Place. "I've never seen so many butterflies!" she exclaimed. "Look—they're even landing on people!" On the way out, Maggie noticed a big mirror in the hallway. She looked at herself.

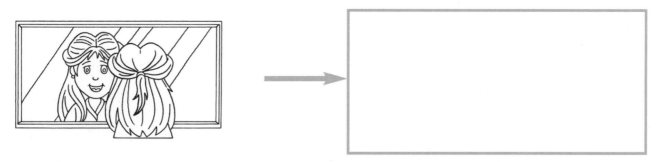

Why Bears Have Short Tails

Read each part of the story. Look at each underlined clue. Then write what you think will happen next.

   The first bear, Bear, had a long, fluffy tail. "Look at my magnificent tail!" Bear told everyone who would listen. One winter day, the animals grew tired of Bear's bragging and went to see Fox. <u>Fox was a clever fellow</u>.

My Prediction: _____

_____

_____

   The next day, Bear spied Fox sitting on a frozen lake by a hole in the ice. Fox was surrounded by fish. "That's a lot of fish," Bear exclaimed.

   "You can catch lots of fish, too," replied Fox. "Put your tail in the water and wait." Bear did as he was told and soon fell asleep. As he slept, <u>the water in the hole started to freeze</u>.

My Prediction: _____

_____

_____

A few hours later, Fox tapped Bear's arm. "Bear!" he shouted. "There's a fish on your tail!" Bear woke up and pulled on his tail, but it was frozen! <u>He pulled again</u>.

My Prediction: _____

_____

Assessment

Read the beginning of the story. Use story clues to predict what will happen next. Write the clues and prediction below.

"Thank you for coming in today," said Ms. Linn. "Molly was doing well in math, but lately her grades have dropped. I've noticed she's not doing her homework."

"I've been watching *Animals in the Wild* on TV," Molly admitted. "I want to be a zookeeper someday, so I'm trying to learn all I can about animals."

"Let's make a new rule," said Dad. "You can watch *Animals in the Wild* until I get home from work. Then, you'll do your math homework. That way, I'll be there if you need any help."

"That sounds like a good plan," said Ms. Linn. "And remember—we have an important math test next week.

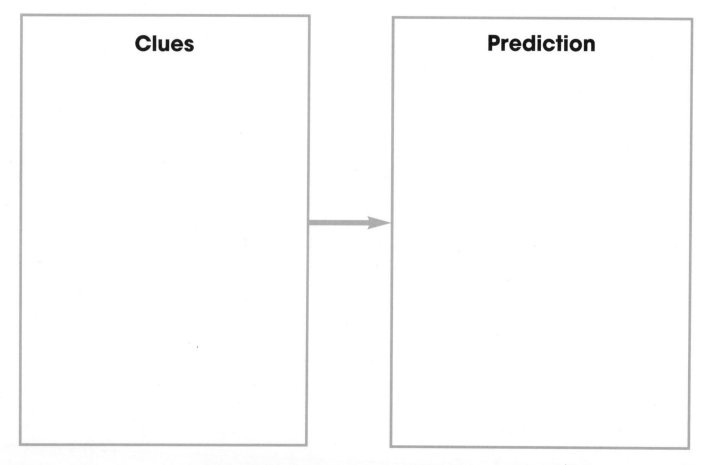

Clues	**Prediction**

Overview Making Predictions in Nonfiction

Directions and Sample Answers for Activity Pages

Day 1	See "Provide a Real-World Example" below.
Day 2	Read the parts of the log together. Discuss the underlined clues. Then ask students to circle the best prediction. (**First:** There will be an eruption. **Second:** Hot rocks and ash will fly out of the volcano. **Third:** The lava flow will bury everything in its path.)
Day 3	Read and discuss each part of the passage. Then ask students to complete the sentences. (**First:** a cavity. **Second:** fewer cavities. **Third:** more cavities.)
Day 4	Read and discuss the passage together. Then ask students to color the circle in front of the best prediction and each piece of evidence. (**Prediction:** The bully will chase the other male hummers away from the feeder. **Evidence:** The male hummer is a bully. The male hummer guards his territory. The male hummer waits for other males to approach his feeder.)
Day 5	Read the passage together. Ask students to use the evidence in the passage to make a prediction and record their ideas on their graphic organizers. Afterward, meet individually with students to discuss their results. Use their responses to plan further instruction and review. (**Evidence:** The first time the dog sits, the trainer uses the clicker and then gives the dog a treat. The trainer keeps repeating this procedure. Soon the dog learns that the sound of the clicker means a treat for sitting. **Prediction:** The dog will sit.)

Provide a Real-World Example

◆ Hand out the Day 1 activity page.

◆ **Say:** *This morning, I got a call from a friend. Then she said she had to go. Her dog had just dropped his leash on the floor in front of her. I predicted, or made a good guess, that she would soon head out the door to walk the dog. I used the clues my friend told me and what I already know about dogs to make my prediction.*

◆ Ask students to locate this prediction on their activity page. Then have them Think/Pair/Share other predictions you could have made.

◆ **Say:** *My cousin got a call from his basketball buddy. His friend won two free tickets to the basketball game next Tuesday night. Think about the clues and what you already know. What do you predict might happen?*

◆ Allow time for students to write their predictions and share them with the group. Then explain that they can also make predictions when they read. Write the following on chart paper:

Making Predictions in Nonfiction

Find evidence in the passage and pictures.

Think about what you already know.

Think about what usually happens.

Think about what you expect to happen and why.

Phone Calls

Look at each picture. Then draw your predictions.

I predict that my friend will soon head out the door to walk her dog.

_____

I predict _____

_____

Volcano Watch

**Read each part of the volcano scientist's log.
Look at the underlined evidence. Then circle
what you think will happen next.**

May 10, 4:15 P.M.

   We've been keeping a close eye on the volcano.
We fear it might erupt, and we want to warn the
people who live nearby. A few minutes ago, we
<u>heard rumbling and felt the ground shake</u>.

What do you predict will happen next?
There will be a thunderstorm.
There will be an eruption.

August 23, 10:02 A.M.

   We <u>saw steam and a smoky cloud of gas</u> coming from the volcano.
Then we <u>heard a thunderous blast</u>.

What do you predict will happen next?
Hot rocks and ash will fly out of the volcano.
The steam and cloud of gas will disappear.

August 23, 10:05 A.M.

   Fire is shooting into the air. Masses of hot lava are creeping down the sides of
the erupting volcano. Thankfully, we've evacuated the area, as many <u>houses and
buildings are in the path of the huge lava flow</u>.

What do you predict will happen next?
The lava will flow around most things in its path.
The lava will bury everything in its path.

Preventing Cavities

Read each part of the passage. Then complete the sentence to predict what you think might happen.

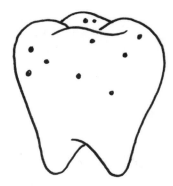

Taking care of your teeth is an important part of good health. A substance called plaque can form on your teeth. If you do not remove the plaque, tiny holes will appear on the surface of your teeth. These tiny holes usually grow bigger.

If I have tiny holes on my teeth, I predict that I may get _____ .

Brushing your teeth frequently helps remove plaque from the tops and sides of your teeth. Flossing is another way to take good care of your teeth. Floss is a special kind of string you pull between your teeth.

If I brush and floss every day, I predict that I will have _____ .

Your teeth will be happy if you keep sugar away from them. When you eat sugary foods and drink sugary sodas, acid develops in your mouth and attacks your teeth. Eventually, one or more of your teeth start to hurt.

If I have lots of sugary foods and drinks, I predict that I will have _____ .

Hummers

Read the passage.

Hummingbirds, sometimes called hummers, are the smallest birds on earth. A hummer is the only bird that can fly both forward and backward. Since its wings beat about 70 times per second, they really do hum! Hummers prefer to fly or sit. They don't like to walk because they have weak feet.

The male hummer is a handsome bird with brightly colored feathers. However, he is a bully. When he finds a feeder, it becomes his territory and he guards it fiercely. The bully hummer will sit and wait for other males to approach "his" feeder.

Color the circle in front of the best prediction.

○ The bully will fly backward when other male hummers approach.

○ The bully will chase the other male hummers away from the feeder.

○ Other hummers will walk away from the feeder when they see the bully.

Color the circle in front of each piece of evidence from the passage.

○ The male hummer is a bully.

○ Some male hummers are not bullies.

○ The male hummer guards his territory.

○ Hummers prefer to find their own food rather than eat from feeders.

○ Hummers scare off bullies by making a humming sound with their wings.

○ The male hummer waits for other males to approach his feeder.

Assessment

Read the passage. Use evidence from the passage to predict what will happen next. Write the evidence and prediction below.

Clicker training is one way to train animals such as dogs, cats, and horses. A clicker is a hand-held device that makes a clicking sound. The trainer decides what the animal needs to learn and then clicks the tool each time the animal performs the task.

For example, a trainer may want to teach a dog to sit. The first time the dog sits, the trainer uses the clicker and then gives the dog a treat. The trainer keeps repeating this procedure, and soon the dog learns that the sound of the clicker means a treat for sitting. What do you predict will happen when the trainer uses the clicker with the dog the next day?

Evidence	**Prediction**

Overview Identifying Sequence of Events in Fiction

Directions and Sample Answers for Activity Pages

Day 1	See "Provide a Real-World Example" below.
Day 2	Read and discuss the story. Then ask students to write signal words from the box to show the sequence of events. (**1:** First. **2:** Then. **3:** Before. **4:** Soon. **5:** Finally.)
Day 3	Read and discuss the story. Then ask students to circle the best answers. (**1:** Kevin put three quarters in his coat pocket. **2:** Mom drove Kevin to school. **3:** Kevin found his quarters.)
Day 4	Read and discuss the story. Then ask students to record the missing events in the boxes. (**Box 2:** peeks out window. **Box 5:** hears laughing. **Box 6:** sees brother.)
Day 5	Read the story together. Ask students to record the main events in order on their graphic organizers. Afterward, meet individually with students to discuss their results. Use their responses to plan further instruction and review. (**Box 1:** The family picks blueberries. **Box 2:** They fill two baskets with berries. **Box 3:** Someone weighs the berries. **Box 4:** Dad pays for the berries. **Box 5:** Mo eats blueberries on his cereal.)

Provide a Real-World Example

◆ Hand out the Day 1 activity page.

◆ **Say:** *Imagine I have three errands to do. I need to go to the grocery store. I need to gas up my car. I also need to take some newspapers to the recycling center. In what sequence, or order, should I do these errands?* Discuss that you should probably gas up the car first so you'll have fuel to drive to the other places.

◆ Have students locate the underlined word *First*. Explain that *first* is a signal word that shows the sequence of events. Read the sentence together, and then ask students to put a 1 in the box for the matching picture.

◆ Repeat the process, having students use the signal words *next* and *after that* to order the other errands. Allow time for students to share their reasons for ordering the events as they did.

◆ Explain that they can also identify sequence of events when they read stories. Write the following on chart paper:

Identifying Sequence of Events in Fiction

Find clues in the story and pictures.

Find words that tell about order, such as *first, next, before, finally, soon, then,* and *after that*.

Think about the order in which things usually happen.

Running Errands

Listen. First, number the pictures in the correct order. Then complete the statements below.

 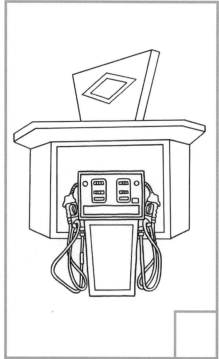 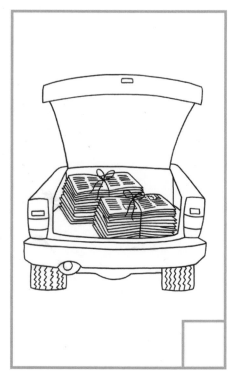

First, I will stop at the gas station.

Next, I will _____

_____.

After that, I will _____.

_____

All Aboard!

Read the story. Then write signal words from the box to show the sequence of events.

Before	Finally
First	Soon	Then

Grandpa and I waited by the tracks. (1)_____, I heard several short whistles. (2)_____, the 2:15 train chugged to a stop. "It's time to board!" Grandpa exclaimed.

(3)_____ getting on the train, Grandpa and I had to show the conductor our tickets. I followed Grandpa down the aisle of a very long car. "Here are our seats. You can sit by the window," Grandpa said.

(4)_____, the train was whizzing by small towns, factories, and farms. People waved at the train, and I waved back.

(5)_____, the conductor announced "Cincinnati O-HI-O"! I looked out the window. There was Grandma!

Three Quarters

**Read the story. Then draw a circle around
the best answer to each question.**

"Time to leave for school!" called Kevin's mom. Kevin
put three quarters in his coat pocket for the pencil machine at
school. Then he ran to the apartment parking lot.

"It snowed last night . . . we'll need to brush the windows,"
said Mom. Mom took brushes from the trunk, and Kevin helped
her sweep off the car.

Mom drove Kevin to school, and he walked to the office to buy some pencils.
His coat pocket was empty! Next, he looked in the pocket of his jeans. Then, he
looked in the school hallway. But he did not find his coins. "You can have one of
my pencils," said his friend Jon.

Finally, school was over, and Kevin walked home. When he got to the parking
lot, he ran to the spot where Mom had parked the night before. "My quarters!" he
exclaimed.

1. What happened first?
Kevin ran to the apartment parking lot.
Kevin put three quarters in his coat pocket.
Mom took brushes from the trunk.

2. What happened right after Kevin and Mom swept snow off the car?
Kevin looked in the school hallway.
Kevin noticed that his coat pocket was empty.
Mom drove Kevin to school.

3. What happened last?
Kevin found his quarters.
School was over.
Jon gave Kevin a pencil.

Scratching at the Window

Read the story. Then write in the empty boxes to show the sequence of events.

S-c-r-a-t-c-h . . . s-c-r-a-t-c-h . . . s-c-r-a-t-c-h. Sasha looked up from her reading. "I don't know what that sound is, but I'm going to find out!" she said.

First, Sasha put her ear against the window and listened. But she couldn't tell what, or who, might be making the strange sound. Next, she pulled the curtain aside and peeked out. But it was too dark to see anything.

"I know!" said Sasha. She tiptoed to the hall closet, found a flashlight, and crept back to the bedroom. As soon as she turned on the flashlight, she heard laughing. Then, she saw her brother outside, running away from the window.

"I should have known!" Sasha exclaimed.

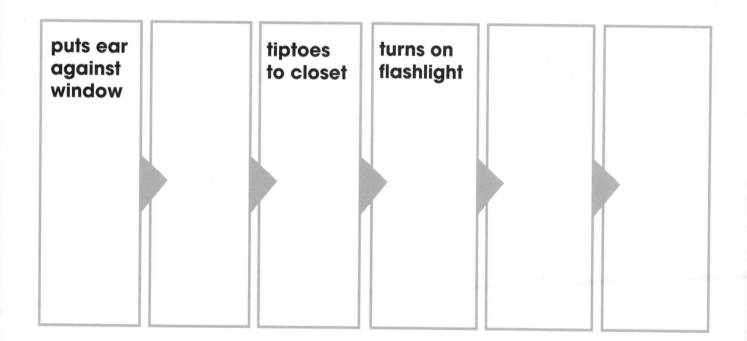

puts ear against window		tiptoes to closet	turns on flashlight		

Assessment

**Read the story. Then fill in the boxes
with the correct order of the main events.**

   "I can't wait to go to Blueberry Hill
Farm with my family!" exclaimed Mo.
"We haven't been there since last summer."

   "What do you do there?" asked Sara.

   "First, we all pick as many berries as we can," replied Mo. "I usually pick the
most, even though I eat a few as I'm picking. After our family has filled two big
baskets with blueberries, someone working at the farm weighs the berries. Then,
Dad pays for the amount of berries we've picked."

   "I've already figured out what you do the next day," said Sara. "You eat LOTS of
blueberries on top of your cereal for breakfast!"

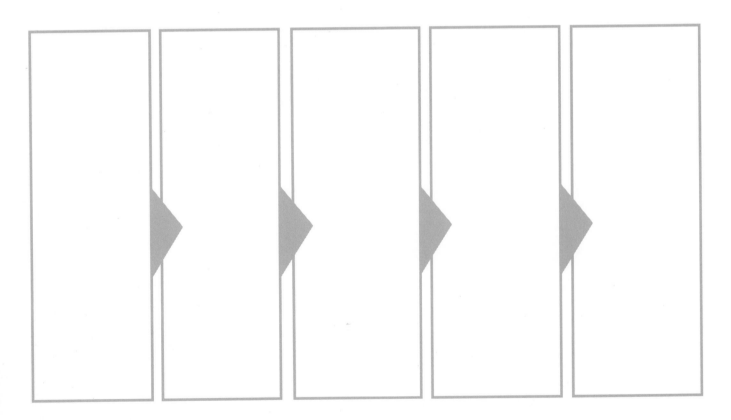

Overview Identifying Sequence of Events in Nonfiction

Directions and Sample Answers for Activity Pages

Day 1	See "Provide a Real-World Example" below.
Day 2	Read and discuss the newspaper article. Then ask students to underline the sequence-of-events signal words and answer the questions. (**Signal Words: as, later, then, soon, immediately, finally. 1:** He noticed red bumps on his leg. **2:** The hiker's leg began to itch. **3:** He had a rash from a poison ivy plant. **4:** The rash finally disappeared.)
Day 3	Read and discuss the passage. Then ask students to write signal words from the box to show the correct sequence of the steps. (**1:** First. **2:** Next. **3:** Then. **4:** After that. **5:** Finally. **6:** Before you go. **Note:** Some answers may vary.)
Day 4	Read and discuss the passage. Then ask students to record the missing events in the boxes. (**Box 2:** floated the blocks to Giza on the Nile River. **Box 4:** pushed the blocks of stone up ramps. **Box 5:** put the blocks in place on the pyramid.)
Day 5	Read the passage together. Ask students to think about the main events in the life of Charles Schulz and record them in order on their graphic organizers. Afterward, meet individually with students to discuss their results. Use their responses to plan further instruction and review. (**Box 1:** took art course by mail. **Box 2:** joined army. **Box 3:** got job in St. Paul. **Box 4:** created own comic strip. **Box 5:** newspaper published *Peanuts*. **Box 6:** became a real cartoonist.)

Provide a Real-World Example

◆ Hand out the Day 1 activity page.

◆ **Say:** *Here are some steps for changing a flat tire: Put on a spare tire. Raise the car with a jack. Lower the car. Remove the flat tire. In what sequence, or order, should someone follow these steps?* Discuss that the first step should be to raise the car with a jack because you cannot carry out the other steps until the car is raised.

◆ Have students locate the word *First* on the left side of the page. Remind students that *First* is a signal word that shows the correct order of events. Ask students to draw a line from *First* to *Raise the car with a jack.*

◆ Repeat the process, having students use the signal words *Second, Next,* and *Finally* to order the other steps. Allow time for students to share their reasons for ordering the tasks as they did.

◆ Explain that they can also identify a sequence of events, or steps in a process, when they read. Write the following on chart paper:

Identifying Sequence of Events in Nonfiction

Find evidence in the story and pictures.

Find words that tell about order, such as *first, second, next, before, finally, soon, then, later,* and *after that.*

Think about the order in which things usually happen.

Flat Tire!

Match the signal word to the correct picture.

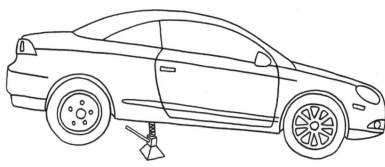

Put on a spare tire.

First

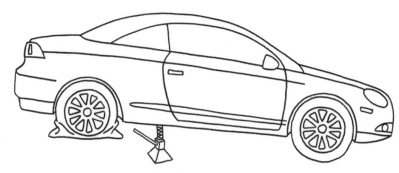

Raise the car with a jack.

Second

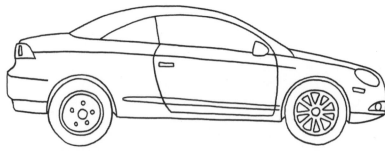

Lower the car.

Next

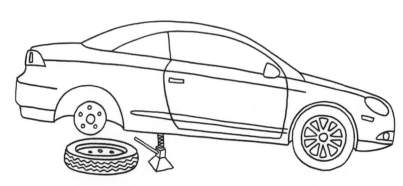

Remove the flat tire.

Finally

Hikers, Beware

**Read the newspaper article. Underline the sequence-of-events
signal words in the passage. Then answer the questions.**

"Poison ivy can be a real threat to hikers," said the president of the local hiking club. He cited a recent incident in which one of the members hiked on a hot day wearing shorts. As he walked, his leg brushed against a plant with three shiny leaves. Later, he noticed red bumps on his leg. Then, his skin began to itch. Soon, the hiker realized he had a rash from a poison ivy plant. The hiker immediately began applying a lotion commonly used to soothe the itching from poison ivy. The rash finally disappeared, but it took three weeks.

"There's a moral to this story," said the club president. "Know your plants, and consider wearing long pants when hiking. Poison ivy is no one's friend!"

1. **What happened after the hiker's leg brushed against a plant with three shiny leaves?** _____

2. **What happened then?** _____

_____

3. **What did the hiker soon realize?** _____

_____

4. **What happened after three weeks passed?** _____

_____

Using a Fireplace

Read the passage. Then write signal words from the box to show the sequence of events.

After that	**Before you go**
Finally	**Next**
First	**Then**

Many homes and vacation spots have fireplaces to keep people warm in winter. The owner of a ski lodge offers the following tips for building a warm, cozy fire.

(1)_____, make sure the top of the chimney is open. (2)_____, put a few crumpled sheets of newspaper in the grate. (3)_____, put flat strips of wood, or kindling, on top of the crumpled paper.

(4)_____, carefully add three split logs, arranging them in layers. (5)_____ , strike a long match and light the paper. Beautiful orange, blue, and red flames should appear.

(6)_____, block the opening of the fireplace with a fireplace screen. This will help keep the people who are enjoying the fire safe.

Building a Pyramid

Read the passage. Then write in the empty boxes to show the sequence of events.

Ancient Egyptians built pyramids as tombs for some of their rulers. The most famous pyramids in Egypt are those at Giza. Although no one knows for sure, some historians believe it took 20,000 to 30,000 workers to build these pyramids. They think the workers first cut huge blocks of stone from limestone pits far away from Giza. Then, other workers floated these blocks to Giza on the Nile River. The next task was to polish the stones. After that, the strongest workers pushed the heavy polished blocks of stone up ramps and put them in place on the pyramid.

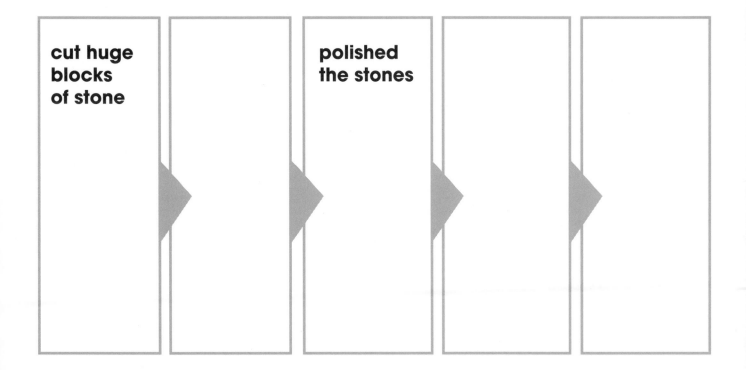

| cut huge blocks of stone | | polished the stones | | |

Assessment

Read the passage. Then fill in the boxes to show the correct order of events.

When Charles Schulz was a young boy in Minnesota, he already knew he wanted to be a cartoonist. After he finished high school, he took an art course by mail. Then, he joined the army.

After his army days, Schulz came home to Minnesota and got a job drawing cartoons for a newspaper in St. Paul. But Charles Schulz had ideas for a comic strip of his own. Soon, he created a strip called *Li'l Folks*.

Before long, a newspaper company published his comic strip with the new name *Peanuts*. Finally, Charles Schulz was a real cartoonist. *Peanuts* was an enormous success. People all over the world loved Charlie Brown, Snoopy, and the other *Peanuts* characters.

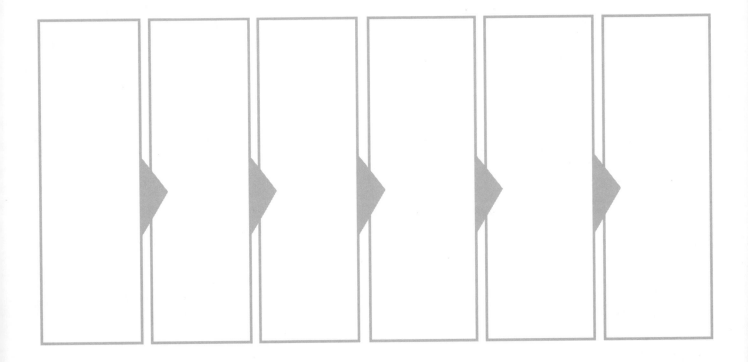

Overview Analyzing Story Elements: Setting

Directions and Sample Answers for Activity Pages

Day 1	See "Provide a Real-World Example" below.
Day 2	Read and discuss the story. Then ask students to answer the questions. (**1:** at an ice hockey game. **2:** team, rink, uniforms, helmets, number 22, padding, gloves, stick, players, referee, puck. **3:** during Thanksgiving. **4:** holiday, turkey, pumpkin pie.)
Day 3	Read and discuss the story and setting clues. Then ask students to circle the best answers. (**1:** in a living room. **Clues:** carpet, game table, sofa. **2:** in the future. **Clues:** beamed himself, pod, Talking Chess, robots.)
Day 4	Read and discuss the story. Then ask students to complete the sentence and color the circle in front of each setting clue from the story. (on a lake in the fall. **Clues:** wood duck, canoeing, beaver dam, cool air, frog, red and gold leaves, water, loon.)
Day 5	Read the story together. Ask students to use clues in the story to figure out the setting and record their ideas on their graphic organizers. Afterward, meet individually with students to discuss their results. Use their responses to plan further instruction and review. (**Clues:** students, girls on left and boys on right, youngest in front and oldest in back, log walls, bench, coal stove, slate, dirt floor. **Setting:** a schoolhouse in pioneer days.)

Provide a Real-World Example

◆ Hand out the Day 1 activity page.

◆ **Say:** *My aunt sent a postcard from a sandy, hot place. She saw lizards and jack rabbits. The card has a photo of some cactuses. Where was my aunt? When do you think she was there?* Discuss clues that help students figure out that your aunt was visiting a desert in the summer. Explain that where and when something takes place is called a setting. Allow time for students to write on the lines to name the setting.

◆ **Say:** *Later, my aunt sent another postcard. This one was from a snowy place with glaciers and mountains. She saw bears, moose, eagles, and whales. The card has a photo of a dogsled race. Where was my aunt? When do you think she was there?* Discuss clues that help students figure out that your aunt was visiting Alaska in the winter. Allow time for them to record their ideas.

◆ Explain that they can also analyze settings when they read stories. Write the following on chart paper:

Analyzing Story Elements: Setting

Find clues in the story and pictures.

Find words that describe a place.

Find words that tell about a time.

Think about when and where an event could happen.

Postcards

Look at each postcard. Then describe the setting.

Where? _____

When? _____

Where? _____

When? _____

Cheers for Number 22!

Read the story. Then answer the questions.

"I'm so glad you got to come home for the holiday," said Dad. "I'm sorry our seats are in the last row, though."

"It's no problem—I can see the rink," said Mei. "I'm just glad to be here! This should be almost as good as the turkey and pumpkin pie Mom is serving tomorrow!"

Mei cheered as the team entered the rink. All the players looked alike in their red uniforms and helmets. Then she spied her brother. "There he is—number 22!" she exclaimed. "He looks like a giant with all that padding on his shoulders, elbows, and legs!"

"Even his hands are giant with those gloves on," agreed Dad. "Sometimes I wonder how he can even hold the stick."

The players quickly took their positions. The referee dropped the puck. "Here we go!" exclaimed Mei.

1. **Where does the story take place?** _____

2. **What clues did you use to answer question 1?** _____

_____

3. **When could the story have taken place?** _____

4. **What clues did you use to answer question 3?** _____

_____

Talking Chess

**Read the story. Draw a line under the setting clues.
Then draw a circle around the best answer to each question.**

"Mom, where are you?" Chip called, as he beamed himself into the pod. "I invited some friends over to play Talking Chess."

"OK," said Mom. "You can play in here. I'm almost done cleaning."

Chip almost tripped over the WhizVac robot moving across the carpet. Another robot was dusting the floating game table in front of the sofa. Mom turned to the last robot. "Set up the chess board for Chip and his friends, please," she requested.

"Speaking of chess, I think we need to get a new set," Chip said. "The last time I played, Knight the Great told me he didn't feel like moving!"

1. Where does the story take place?

    in a dining room   in a living room   on a porch

2. When does the story take place?

    long ago   in the present day   in the future

Two in a Canoe

**Read the story. Complete the sentence.
Then color the circle in front of each
setting clue from the story.**

    "I love canoeing," said Mary.
"And it's a perfect day for it. The
cool air feels great."

    Her twin brother Larry nodded.
"I've taken lots of great pictures, too," he said. "I got a shot of the red and gold
leaves of the trees by the edge of the water."

    "Listen! Did you hear that frog?" asked Mary. "I hear a loon, too."

    "Look! There's a wood duck," said Larry. "Let's try to paddle closer so I can get a
picture. Oops—scared him away!"

    "No matter . . . here's another great picture," said Mary. "A beaver dam!"

This story takes place on _____ **in** _____.

Setting Clues

○ wood duck   ○ Mary   ○ lots of great pictures

○ twin brother   ○ cool air   ○ water

○ canoeing   ○ frog   ○ loon

○ beaver dam   ○ red and gold leaves   ○ perfect day

Assessment

**Read the story. Then fill in the boxes
to show the setting.**

Sarah and the other girls sat on the left side of the room, and the boys sat on the right. The youngest students sat in the front, and the oldest students sat in back with Sarah.

Suddenly, the wind whistled through the cracks in the log walls. "Brr . . ." Sarah whispered to her friend Rebecca. "I wish our bench was closer to the coal stove." As Rebecca nodded, she dropped her slate. Sarah picked it up from the dirt floor and blew off the dust.

"Thank you, Sarah," said their teacher, Miss Whittington. "Rebecca will need her slate to copy the poem from the board. I'll expect everyone to have it memorized for class tomorrow."

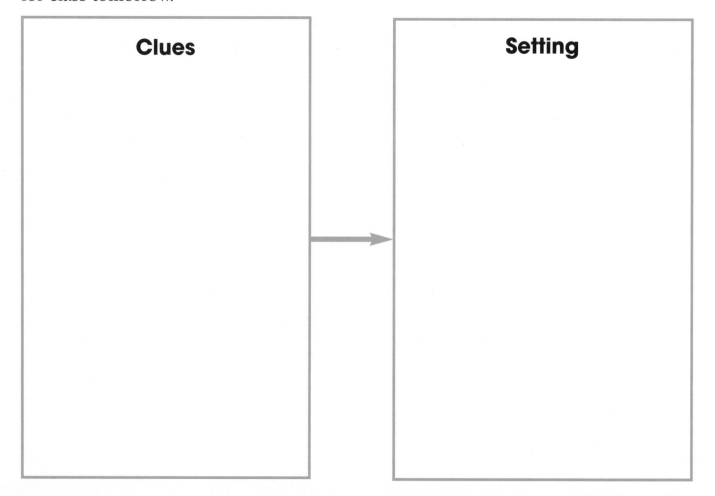

Clues	Setting

Overview Analyzing Story Elements: Plot

Directions and Sample Answers for Activity Pages

Day 1	See "Provide a Real-World Example" below.
Day 2	Read and discuss the story. Then ask students to read the questions and write or draw their answers. (**Beginning:** Dora and her mom have tickets to a play, but they're having guests. **Middle:** Give the tickets away. Try to exchange them. Get tickets for the cousins, too. **End:** Mom and Dora get tickets for the cousins.)
Day 3	Read and discuss the story. Then ask students to circle the best answers. (**1:** Nina and Jason already had the gifts they got for their birthdays. **2:** Nina and Jason swapped their gifts.)
Day 4	Read and discuss the story. Then ask students to write answers to the questions. (**1:** Anthony. **2:** The library will be closed when Anthony can go. **3:** Anthony will write his report without going to the library. **4:** The report may not be as good as it could have been. Anthony may have to rewrite it.)
Day 5	Read the story together. Ask students to record the problem and solution on their graphic organizers. Afterward, meet individually with students to discuss their results. Use their responses to plan further instruction and review. (**Problem:** Dad's car is stuck in a snow bank. **Solution:** Dig snow from around the wheels. Sprinkle sand around the wheels. Work together to push the car.)

Provide a Real-World Example

◆ Hand out the Day 1 activity page.

◆ **Say:** *A school librarian found out that painters were coming the next week. What problem could this cause? How could the librarian solve the problem?*

◆ Discuss that no one may be allowed to enter the library to get books while the painters are there. One solution could be to ask students to help move some of the books to another place in the building. Invite students to Think/Pair/Share other problems and solutions and then write their ideas on the lines. Then repeat the process with a second scenario, in which five people want to watch a movie in a room with one sofa and one chair.

◆ **Say:** *These situations are like the plot of a story. A story has a problem and solution to make it interesting to read.* Write the following on chart paper:

Analyzing Story Elements: Plot

Read the beginning to find out the problem.

Read the middle to see what the characters do.

Read the end to see how the characters solve the problem.

Problems

Listen to each problem. Then think about possible solutions.

Problem: _____

Solution: _____

Problem: _____

Solution: _____

The Cousins Are Coming

Read the story. Then read the questions and write or draw your answers.

"I just got an e-mail," said Mom. "Your cousins are coming to spend the weekend!"

"Yeah!" said Dora. "That sounds like fun." Then she frowned. "Uh-oh . . . we have tickets to the play on Saturday night."

"Hmm . . ." said Mom. "What shall we do?"

"We could give our tickets away," said Dora. "We could try to exchange them. Or we could get tickets for my cousins, too. I think they'd love the play!"

Mom called the box office. Then she turned to Dora. "We're in luck!" she said. "We were able to get tickets for all the cousins. And they were half-price, too!"

Reread the beginning of the story. What is the problem?

Reread the middle of the story. What ideas does Dora have to solve the problem?

Reread the end of the story. How do Dora and Mom solve their problem?

Happy Birthday!

Read the story. Then draw a circle around the best answer to each question.

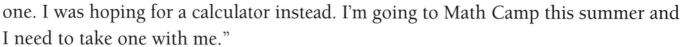

Jason and Nina had the same birthday. The next day, Jason called Nina. "Hi! Did you have a nice birthday?" he asked.

"Yes!" said Nina. "The only thing is, my Uncle Ben sent me a microscope, and I already have one. I was hoping for a calculator instead. I'm going to Math Camp this summer and I need to take one with me."

"Really?" said Jason. "My Aunt Beatrice sent me a calculator, but I already have one. I'd love a microscope! Science is my favorite subject, you know, and I'm planning on collecting some new rock specimens over the summer."

"Let's swap gifts!" said Nina. "Then we'll both have exactly what we need."

"Great idea!" said Jason. "You just bumped up the *Happy* in my *Happy Birthday*!"

1. What is the problem in the story?

Nina and Jason did not know each other.
Nina and Jason already had the gifts they got for their birthdays.
Nina and Jason did not like the gifts they got for their birthdays.

2. What is the solution to the problem?

Nina borrowed the calculator from Jason.
Jason bought the microscope from Nina.
Nina and Jason swapped their gifts.

Anthony's Dilemma

Read the story. Then answer each question.

"My Saturday dog-walking business is going great!" said Anthony. "Tomorrow I have three appointments. I'm walking Zorro from 10 to 11. I'm walking Pug from 11:15 to 12:15. Then, I'm walking Daisy from 12:30 to 1:30."

"What about your report on dinosaurs?" asked Dad. "It's due Monday morning. Don't you need to go to the library tomorrow?"

"Yes," said Anthony. "I'll go after I finish walking Daisy."

"The library closes at noon tomorrow," said Dad.

"Oh, well," said Anthony. "I already know a lot about dinosaurs. I'll just write my report without going to the library."

1. Who has a problem? _____

2. What is the problem? _____

3. What is the character's solution to the problem? _____

_____

4. What new problem could this solution cause? _____

_____

Assessment

**Read the story. Then fill in the boxes with the
problem and solution.**

"Whirrr . . . whirrrr . . ." The wheels of the car
spun, throwing clumps of snow into the chilly air.

"It won't go forward, and it won't go back," said
Dad. "I wasn't expecting a snow bank in our own
driveway this morning!"

"Maybe I can help," said Gina. She got a shovel and dug the snow out from
around the wheels. The car moved a little, but not enough.

"This might help," said Mr. Bowers from next door. He brought over a bag of
sand. Dad and Gina sprinkled the sand around the wheels. The car moved a little
more, but still not enough.

Just then, a group of teenagers walked by. "We'll help!" they said. Dad got back
in the car to steer, and everyone else pushed. Soon, the car was in the street.

"Thanks!" said Dad. "Let me know when I can help all of YOU sometime!"

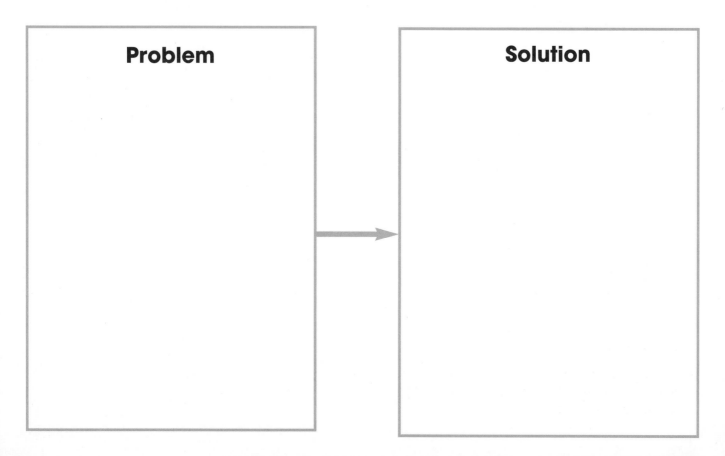

Overview Analyzing Character: Traits and Feelings

Directions and Sample Answers for Activity Pages

Day 1	See "Provide a Real-World Example" below.
Day 2	Read and discuss the story. Then ask students to answer the questions. (Answers will vary, but could include **1:** fun-loving. **2:** excited. **3:** fussy. **4:** nervous.)
Day 3	Read and discuss the story. Then ask students to circle the words that best describe the characters' traits and feelings. (**1:** unhappy. **2:** kind. **3:** frightened. **4:** ungrateful.)
Day 4	Read and discuss the story. Then ask students to circle the best answers. (**1:** Hannah is musical. **2:** Hannah squirms in her seat. **3:** Hannah is friendly. **4:** Hannah feels annoyed. **5:** Dad says Hannah knows her piece by heart.)
Day 5	Read the story together. Ask students to write about Tanya's traits and feelings on their graphic organizers. Afterward, meet individually with students to discuss their results. Use their responses to plan further instruction and review. (**Clues:** won school and city spelling bees; **Trait:** intelligent. **Clues:** studied word lists every evening, learned to spell 50 new words every week, wrote hardest words on cards to practice; **Traits:** hard-working, organized. **Clues:** couldn't eat breakfast, stomach doing flip-flops; **Feelings:** anxious, nervous. **Clues:** shouting, ready for pancakes; **Feelings:** happy, relieved.)

Provide a Real-World Example

◆ Hand out the Day 1 activity page.

◆ **Say:** *I recently heard about a boy who fell onto some railroad tracks. A man ran to the boy as fast as he could. He grabbed the boy and pulled him off the tracks just before a train roared by.*

◆ Write the words **traits** and **feelings** on the board. **Say:** *A **trait** is a special quality about a person. It is the way a person usually is. I can think of a trait that describes the man who rescued the boy. The man is brave.* Allow time for students to write this trait beside the picture of the man and share others they think apply. Then **say:** *A **feeling** is something that changes with the situation. What feelings do you think the boy experienced during his rescue?* Allow time for students to share their ideas and write them on the page.

◆ Explain that students can also analyze a character's traits and feelings when they read stories. Write the following on chart paper:

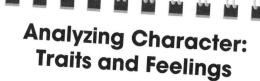

Analyzing Character: Traits and Feelings

Find clues in the pictures and words.

Think about what a character thinks, says, and does.

Think of words that describe the character.

Think of words that describe how the character feels.

Rescued!

Listen to the example. Then write the traits and feelings for each character.

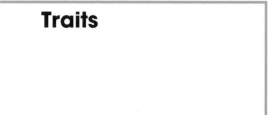

Traits

Feelings

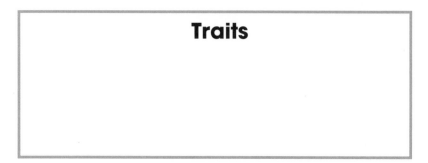

Traits

Feelings

Top of the City

Read the story. Then answer each question.

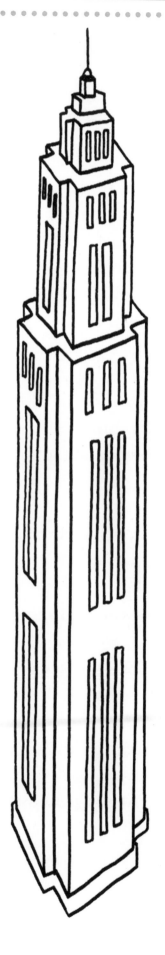

"Bye, Mom!" said Kate and Lucy. They caught up with Dad at the bus stop. Kate adjusted her sunglasses—the big ones with blue eyeballs on the lenses.

"Your hair is sticking out," said Lucy.

"I don't care," said Kate. "At least I didn't make Mom braid mine twice like you did!"

"I didn't like the way it looked the first time," said Lucy.

Soon, the bus arrived at the tallest building in the city. Kate and Lucy follow Dad to the elevator for a ride to the top.

"I've always wanted to ride in one of these glass elevators," exclaimed Kate. "Look down there at the little cars and tiny people."

Lucy covered her eyes. "Dad, stop the elevator! I feel sick," she moaned.

"Hang in there," Dad says. "We'll be at the top soon."

1. What is Kate like? _____

_____

2. How does Kate feel? _____

_____

3. What is Lucy like? _____

_____

4. How does Lucy feel? _____

_____

Tiger in the Hole

Read the story. Then draw a circle around the word that belongs in each blank.

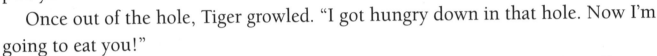

All the villagers were afraid of Tiger. To keep him away, they dug deep holes around the village. One day, a stranger saw Tiger at the bottom of a hole. "Please, please help me," Tiger sobbed.

"Grab this branch," the stranger replied. "I'll pull you out."

Once out of the hole, Tiger growled. "I got hungry down in that hole. Now I'm going to eat you!"

The stranger saw Tiger's sharp teeth and began shaking. "Let's ask the village judge if that's fair," he suggested.

Tiger and the stranger found the judge. "Show me what happened," she said.

Tiger walked back to the hole and jumped in. The stranger got a branch. But before he could pull Tiger out, the judge told him to go on his way. "This man tried to save you," the judge said to Tiger. "Now you'll have plenty of time to think about your actions."

1. **At the beginning of the story, Tiger feels _____.**   pleased   unhappy

2. **The stranger is _____.**   kind   bossy

3. **When Tiger is out of the hole, the stranger feels _____.**   frightened   relieved

4. **The judge knows that Tiger is _____.**   thoughtful   ungrateful

Tryouts Today

Read the story. Then draw a circle around the best answer to each question.

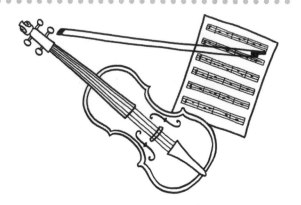

Hannah read the sign: **Tryouts Today**. "This must be the right place," she told Dad.

Hannah and Dad found seats in the back of the auditorium. A boy was playing his violin on the stage. "Wow, he's really good," Hannah said.

Hannah squirmed in her seat as she watched several other kids try out. "They're ALL good," she said. "Maybe I should have stayed home."

"Then you would have missed the bus ride," Dad teased.

"It WAS fun talking to the kids across the aisle," admitted Hannah. "But I got tired of picking up my sheet music every time the bus hit a pothole."

"You don't need your sheet music anyway," said Dad. "You know your piece by heart. And, by the way, it's your turn!"

1. Hannah is at the tryouts. What trait does this suggest?

  Hannah is organized.   Hannah is musical.

2. Think about how Hannah feels as she waits for her turn. What clue is in the story?

  Hannah squirms in her seat.   Hannah has fun on the bus.

3. Hannah talks with some kids on the bus. What trait does this suggest?

  Hannah is bossy.   Hannah is friendly.

4. Hannah's bus hits some potholes. How did this make Hannah feel?

  Hannah feels worried.   Hannah feels annoyed.

5. Think about how Dad feels when it's Hannah's turn. What clue is in the story?

  Dad says Hannah knows   Dad says all the kids
  her piece by heart.   are good violin players.

Assessment

Read the story. Then fill in the boxes to show at least one trait and one feeling.

Tanya fastened her seat belt and sighed. Then she held up her hand and counted on her fingers. "I won the school spelling bee. I won the city spelling bee. I studied my word lists every evening. I learned to spell fifty new words every week. I wrote the hardest words on cards to practice again and again. So why couldn't I eat my breakfast this morning? And why is my stomach doing flip-flops?"

Mom smiled and patted Tanya's leg. "We'll be at the state bee soon," she said. "Just try to relax."

That afternoon, Mom and Tanya were on their way back home. "Wow! Yea! Hooray!" Tanya shouted again and again. "And, Mom—can we stop for those pancakes now?"

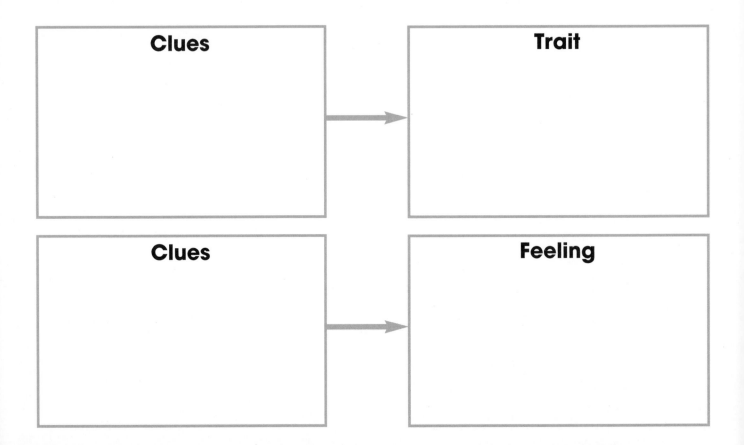

Clues	Trait

Clues	Feeling

Overview Analyzing Character: Relationships and Changes

Directions and Sample Answers for Activity Pages

Day 1	See "Provide a Real-World Example" below.
Day 2	Read and discuss the story. Then ask students to circle the words that belong in the blanks. (**1:** kind. **2:** friends. **3:** ashamed. **4:** clever. **5:** selfish)
Day 3	Read and discuss the story. Then ask students to circle the best answers. (**1:** coach and player. **2:** uninterested. **3:** from easy-going to hardworking. **4:** proud. **5:** "I like the new me!")
Day 4	Read and discuss the story. Then ask students to color the circle in front of each true statement. (Tony and Calvin are cousins. Jen and Calvin are brother and sister. At first, Tony is afraid of horses. At the end of the story, Tony likes horses. At the end of the story, Calvin likes horses.)
Day 5	Read the story together. Ask students to write about Alma's relationships and changes on their graphic organizers. Afterward, meet individually with students to discuss their results. Use their responses to plan further instruction and review. (**Clues:** lived across the street, played with cats; **Relationship:** neighbors. **Clues:** forgets to feed cats, gets up early to feed cats; **Change:** from careless to responsible.)

Provide a Real-World Example

◆ Hand out the Day 1 activity page.

◆ **Say:** *I know two boys who do everything together. They especially like to ride bikes. Recently, both boys took acting classes. They've been in a few videos. They used to hang out with their classmates. But now that they're becoming famous, they often ignore the other kids.*

◆ Write the words *relationships* and *changes* on the board. **Say:** *People have many types of relationships. They can be family members, friends, or neighbors. I think the boys I mentioned are friends, since they do everything together.* Allow time for students to write about this relationship in the box. Then **say:** *People sometimes change as time goes on. They change in many ways and for many reasons. How did these two boys change?* Allow time for students to share their ideas and write them on the page.

◆ Repeat the process for the second set of pictures. Then explain that students can also analyze a character's relationships and changes when they read stories. Write the following on chart paper:

Analyzing Character: Relationships and Changes

Use clues in the pictures and words to figure out . . .

- which characters are in the same family
- which characters are friends or neighbors
- which characters go to the same school or job
- how the characters think, feel, and act at the beginning of the story
- how they think, feel, and act at the end of the story
- what makes them change

Two Boys, Two Girls

Listen to each example. Then describe the relationship and how it changed.

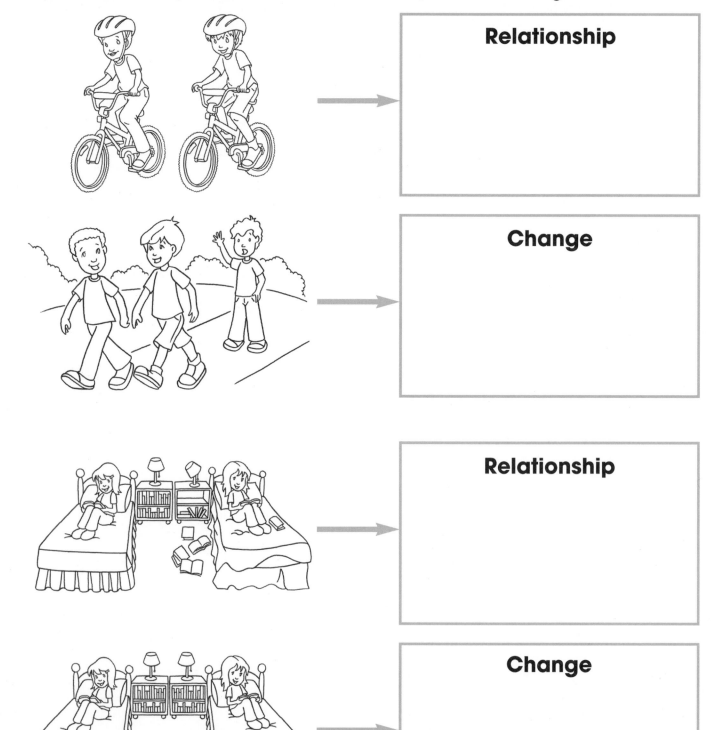

Relationship

Change

Relationship

Change

Why Turkeys Don't Trust Humans

Read the story. Then draw a circle around the word that belongs in each blank.

Turkey Girl took care of the village turkeys. Every morning, she let them out of their cages to search for food. Every evening, she tucked them back in. She talked to them softly and stroked their feathers.

One evening, Turkey Girl told them about a dance in the village. "I wish I could go," she said. "But everyone would laugh at my old, patched clothes."

"We'll help you!" exclaimed the turkeys. They danced around her, brushing her with their wings. Soon, her ragged dress turned into a sparkling gown.

"Oh, thank you!" Turkey Girl cried, running all the way to the dance.

The dance lasted all night and into the next day. Turkey Girl had a wonderful time—so wonderful, in fact, that she forgot to go to the turkey cages the next morning. The hungry turkeys finally broke their way out and ran away, never to be seen again.

1. At the beginning of the story, the girl was _____.   kind   mean

2. Turkey Girl and the turkeys were _____.   friends   strangers

3. Turkey Girl was _____ of her old clothes.   proud   ashamed

**4. The _____ turkeys made a beautiful gown
    for Turkey Girl.**   clever   silly

5. At the end of the story, Turkey Girl was _____.   thoughtful   selfish

Leroy's Decision

Read the story. Then draw a circle around the best answer for each question.

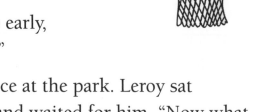

Mr. Rand watched Leroy play basketball in the park. "You're good!" Mr. Rand said. "You can run, jump, pass, dribble, and shoot. Why don't you join the school team?"

"No way!" said Leroy. "I don't want to get up early, work out, and practice. I just want to have fun!"

A few days later, Mr. Rand held a team practice at the park. Leroy sat on the sidelines and watched. Afterward, Mr. Rand waited for him. "Now what do you think?" he asked.

"I want to get up early, work out, and practice!" said Leroy.

After the team's first game, Mr. Rand said, "I like your new basketball skills, Leroy."

"I like the new me!" Leroy replied with a grin.

1. What is the relationship between Mr. Rand and Leroy?

   father and son   coach and player

2. What is Leroy like at the beginning of the story?

   patient   uninterested

3. How does Leroy change?

   from easy-going to hardworking   from unselfish to selfish

4. How does Leroy feel about himself at the end of the story?

   proud   unhappy

5. Which is a clue to how Leroy feels now?

   "I just want to have fun!"   "I like the new me!

Way Too Big

**Read the story. Then color the circle in front of
every statement that is true.**

Tony's mom hung up the phone. "That was
my brother," she said. "Next weekend, we're
going to the ranch. Calvin's looking forward to
seeing you. You boys always have a good time."

"That's cool, Mom. But you know how I feel
about horses. They're WAY too big!"

When Tony's family arrived at the ranch, Calvin immediately took Tony to the
stables. "You won't have any trouble riding Daisy," he said. "She's very gentle. Here,
I'll help you up."

Tony turned away, shuffling his feet, while Calvin waited. Finally, Tony climbed
into the saddle. "OK," he said, "but I'm not leaving the corral."

After a while, Jen came out of the house. "Calvin!" she called. "Dad says lunch
is ready."

As the boys walked to the house, Tony smiled at Calvin. "Can we ride again
after lunch?"

○ **Tony and Calvin are brothers.**

○ **Tony and Calvin are cousins.**

○ **Jen and Calvin are brother and sister.**

○ **Jen and Calvin are cousins.**

○ **At first, Tony is afraid of horses.**

○ **At first, Calvin is afraid of horses.**

○ **At the end of the story, Tony likes horses.**

○ **At the end of the story, Calvin likes horses.**

Assessment

Read the story. Then fill in the boxes to show one relationship and one change.

Ms. Pulaski lived across the street from Alma. Alma liked to play with Ms. Pulaski's cats, Gomer and Gilda.

One Saturday, Alma went to the mall with her mom. "Oh, no!" she shouted as they drove home later that morning. "Ms. Pulaski is away. I was supposed to feed Gomer and Gilda this morning!" Alma rushed to Ms. Pulaski's house the minute she got home. Gomer and Gilda were meowing loudly. "I'm sorry!" Alma said, putting food and water into their bowls.

A few weeks later, Ms. Pulaski called. "Alma, I need to be gone overnight. Will you feed Gomer and Gilda in the morning?"

"I sure will!" said Alma. As soon as she hung up, she set her alarm. Then she found Mom. "I'm going to Ms. Pulaski's house first thing in the morning," Alma said.

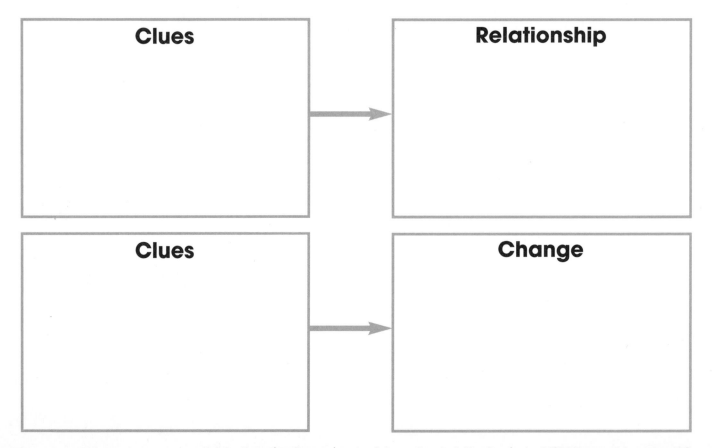

Clues	Relationship

Clues	Change

     Unit 8 • Everyday Comprehension Intervention Activities Grade 4 • ©2010 Newmark Learning, LLC

Overview Identifying Stated Main Idea and Supporting Details

Directions and Sample Answers for Activity Pages

Day 1	See "Provide a Real-World Example" below.
Day 2	Read and discuss the paragraph. Then ask students to draw a circle around the best answers. (**1:** Some people use wind turbines to make electricity. **2:** The blades are connected to a shaft. **3:** A brake keeps the wind from turning the blades too fast.)
Day 3	Read and discuss the paragraph. Then ask students to write the stated main idea and supporting details. (**Stated Main Idea:** These caves have amazing formations on their walls, floors, and ceilings. **Cave popcorn:** little round knobs. **Cave bacon:** colored stripes. **Soda straws:** thin, hollow tubes.)
Day 4	Read and discuss the paragraph. Then ask students to underline the stated main idea and draw a line from the name of each body part to its supporting detail. (**Stated Main Idea:** From head to tail, beavers are made to live in these watery habitats. **Body:** sleek for swimming. **Back feet:** webbed for swimming. **Tail:** flat for steering. **Ears:** close under water. **Front feet:** well suited for scooping mud.)
Day 5	Read the paragraph together. Ask students to record the stated main idea and supporting details. Afterward, meet individually with students to discuss their results. Use their responses to plan further instruction and review. (**Stated Main Idea:** Creating the Mount Rushmore National Memorial was a challenging task. **Supporting Details:** sculptor and 400 workers dynamited, hammered, and drilled into the rock; harsh weather and lack of money delayed work; rock on the Jefferson head cracked; fourteen years of hard work.)

Provide a Real-World Example

◆ Hand out the Day 1 activity page.

◆ **Say:** *A Baltimore oriole is a colorful bird. It has a black head, black wings, and black tail feathers, but the rest of its body is bright orange.* Ask students to complete the main idea you stated. Then ask them to color the first bird according to the supporting details you supplied. Repeat if needed.

◆ **Say:** *Another colorful bird is the red-winged blackbird. It is black with red patches on its shoulders. Each patch has a yellow border.* Again allow time for students to complete the stated main idea and color the bird appropriately.

◆ Explain that they can also find stated main ideas and supporting details when they read. **Say:** *The main idea is the most important statement. The supporting details tell more about the main idea.* Then write the following on chart paper:

Identifying Stated Main Idea and Supporting Details

See what the paragraph is about.

Find the sentence that states the most important idea.

Find details that support, or give more information about, the main idea.

Colorful Birds

Listen to the information. Then complete the stated main idea.

Stated Main Idea: A Baltimore oriole is a _____.

Stated Main Idea: Another colorful bird is the _____.

Wind Machines

**Read the paragraph. Then draw a circle
around the best answer to each question.**

Some people use wind turbines to make electricity.
Most wind turbines have two or three large blades at
the top of a tower. The blades are connected to a shaft.
When wind flows over the blades, they turn and spin
the shaft. The spinning shaft then starts a generator,
which makes electricity. A brake keeps the wind from
turning the blades too fast. High wind speed could
damage the blades or even cause one to break off.

1. **What is the stated main idea of the paragraph?**
   High wind speed could damage the blades.
   Some people use wind turbines to make electricity.
   Blades turn and spin the shaft.

2. **Think about how wind turbines are put together.
   Which is one supporting detail?**
   The blades are connected to a shaft.
   Wind flows over the blades.
   A generator makes electricity.

3. **Think about wind turbines and wind speed.
   Which is one supporting detail?**
   Most wind turbines have two or three large blades.
   A brake keeps the wind from turning the blades too fast.
   A spinning shaft turns on a generator.

Popcorn, Bacon, and Soda Straws

Read the paragraph. Then complete the sentences.

Have you ever visited a limestone cave? These caves have amazing formations on their walls, floors, and ceilings. One formation is called cave popcorn. Water trickles out of the wall and makes little round knobs that look like popcorn. Cave bacon is a formation that looks like bacon. Its colored stripes come from minerals in the water that runs down the wall. Another formation is called soda straws. Water drips from the ceiling, forming thin, hollow tubes that look like the straws people use to sip drinks.

Write the stated main idea.

_____

Write one supporting detail about each formation.

Cave popcorn: _____

Cave bacon: _____

Soda straws: _____

From Head to Tail

**Read the paragraph. Underline the stated main idea.
Then draw a line from the name of each body part to a
supporting detail you learned about it.**

Beavers live on the banks of ponds, rivers,
streams, and lakes. From head to tail, beavers are
made to live in these watery habitats. Diving and
swimming well are important. Beavers are good
swimmers because they have a sleek body shape, webbed back feet, and a flat tail
for steering. Their ears and nose close when they go under water, too. Beavers build
lodges of mud and sticks. Their front feet are well suited for scooping mud.

Parts of a Beaver's Body	**Supporting Details**
body	flat for steering under water
back feet	well suited for scooping
tail	webbed for swimming
ears	sleek for swimming
front feet	close under water

Assessment

Read the paragraph. Then fill in the boxes with the stated main idea and supporting details.

The heads of four presidents of the United States are carved into a mountain in South Dakota: George Washington, Thomas Jefferson, Theodore Roosevelt, and Abraham Lincoln. This colossal sculpture is the Mount Rushmore National Memorial. Creating the Mount Rushmore National Memorial was a challenging task. Sculptor Gutzon Borglum and around 400 workers dynamited, hammered, and drilled into the rock. Harsh weather and lack of money continually delayed their work. Then, the rock on the Jefferson head cracked, and the workers had to start carving it all over again. After fourteen years of hard work, Borglum and the workers finished all four heads. Since then, millions of visitors have marveled at his masterpiece dedicated to some of the greatest leaders in the history of America.

Stated Main Idea	Supporting Details

Overview Identifying Unstated Main Idea and Supporting Details

Directions and Sample Answers for Activity Pages

Day 1	See "Provide a Real-World Example" below.
Day 2	Read and discuss the paragraph. Then ask students to draw a circle around the best answers. (**1:** They explain how scientists named three dinosaurs. **2:** Scientists named some dinosaurs for a body part.)
Day 3	Read and discuss the paragraph. Then ask students to write the supporting details and an unstated main idea. (**Square:** shape, two-dimensional, four equal sides, four equal corners. **Cube:** solid shape, three-dimensional, six equal squares called faces, edges where the sides of the squares meet. **Unstated Main Idea:** A shape and a solid shape are different, but a solid shape can have shapes in it.)
Day 4	Read and discuss the paragraph. Then ask students to color the circle in front of each supporting detail and write an unstated main idea. (**Supporting Details:** Lacy green leaves will sprout from the top. Artichokes are root vegetables. Leave about one-half inch of the stem. Put sand and a little water into a dish. A carrot is a root vegetable. Keep the dish in a sunny spot. Press the bottom of the root into the sand. **Unstated Main Idea:** You can grow a kitchen garden using root vegetables.)
Day 5	Read the paragraph together. Ask students to record the supporting details, figure out what they have in common, and use the information to write the unstated main idea. Afterward, meet individually with students to discuss their results. Use their responses to plan further instruction and review. (**Supporting Details:** hunted for food, trapped in fishing nets, caught in boat propellers, water polluted, nests disturbed. **Unstated Main Idea:** Green sea turtles are in danger.)

Provide a Real-World Example

◆ Hand out the Day 1 activity page.

◆ **Say:** *Some people have pet rabbits. Rabbits are quiet. They keep themselves clean. They can learn to use a litter box.* Ask students to complete these supporting details on the page.

◆ **Say:** *We can figure out what these details have in common and use that information to determine a main idea. Each detail is a good thing about rabbits, so I think the main idea is that rabbits are good pets.* Allow time for students to discuss and write the unstated main idea.

◆ **Say:** *People use fractions when sharing a pizza. People use decimals when shopping. People use skip-counting when telling time.* Allow time for students to complete these supporting details. Then ask them to figure out what the details have in common and determine the unstated main idea. (*People use math every day.*)

◆ Explain that students can also use supporting details to figure out an unstated main idea when they read. Write the following on chart paper:

Identifying Unstated Main Idea and Supporting Details

See what the paragraph is about.

Find details about the topic. Figure out what the details have in common.

Use that information to determine an unstated main idea.

Details, Details

Listen to the information. Then complete the supporting details.

Supporting Details:

Rabbits are _____.

They keep themselves _____.

They can learn to use a _____.

Unstated Main Idea:

Rabbits are _____.

Supporting Details:

People use _____ when
sharing a pizza.
People use _____ when
shopping.
People use _____ when
telling time.

Unstated Main Idea:
People use _____ every day.

Dinosaurs

**Read the paragraph. Then draw a circle
around the best answer to each question.**

Scientists named the dinosaur *Anatosaurus*
for its nose. It had a nose shaped like a duck's
bill, so they used the Latin root "anato"
(meaning "duck") in its name. Scientists
named the dinosaur *Pentaceratops* for its head.
This prehistoric creature had five horns on its
head, so the Greek root "penta" (meaning "five") is part of its name. Scientists
named the dinosaur *Barosaurus* for its long neck. Scientists thought the bones
would make the dinosaur's neck very heavy to lift. Therefore, they used the Greek
root "baro" (meaning "heavy") in its name. As it turns out, the bones were hollow
which made the neck not so heavy after all.

1. What do the details in the paragraph have in common?

They describe the bodies of three dinosaurs.

They explain how scientists named three dinosaurs.

They describe the bones of three dinosaurs.

2. What is the unstated main idea of the paragraph?

Scientists study dinosaur's bones.

Some dinosaurs had horns on their heads.

Scientists named some dinosaurs for a body part.

Squares and Cubes

Read the paragraph. Then write an answer to each question.

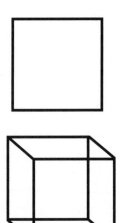

What is the difference between a square and a cube? A square is a shape. It is two-dimensional—it has length and width, but it is flat. It has four equal sides and four equal corners. A cube is a solid shape. It is three-dimensional—it has length, width, and height. It has six equal squares, called faces. It also has edges. The edges are where the sides of the squares meet.

Write supporting details about a square and a cube.

Square: _____

_____

Cube: _____

_____

Write an unstated main idea. _____

_____

Kitchen Garden

**Read the paragraph. Color the circle in front of each
supporting detail. Then write an unstated main idea.**

You can grow a carrot top in a kitchen garden.
You can also grow the tops of other root vegetables,
such as chicory, parsley, and artichokes. Cut off the
leafy green tops so that only about one-half inch of the
stem remains. Then cut the root off about one-half inch
below the stem. Fill a dish with sand, and add a little water. Press the bottom
of the root into the sand. Place the dish in a sunny spot, and add a little water each
day to keep the sand damp. Soon you'll see lacy green leaves sprout from the tops.

Supporting Details:

○ Fill a dish with water.

○ Lacy green leaves will sprout from the top.

○ Artichokes are root vegetables.

○ Many people grow kitchen gardens.

○ Leave about one-half inch of the stem.

○ Leave the leafy green tops.

○ Put sand and a little water into a dish.

○ A carrot is a root vegetable.

○ Press the bottom of the stem into the sand.

○ Keep the dish in a sunny spot.

○ Add a little sand to the dish each day.

○ Press the bottom of the root into the sand.

Unstated Main Idea: _____

_____.

Assessment

**Read the paragraph. Then fill in the boxes with
the supporting details and unstated main idea.**

Many countries have laws against hunting
green sea turtles. However, some turtle hunters
ignore the laws. These hunters kill the turtles
and sell the meat and eggs for food. The green
sea turtle population is also shrinking because of
accidents. Some greens get trapped in fishing nets and drown, and others get
caught in boat propellers. Humans destroy the habitat of greens when they build.
The construction process pollutes the turtles' water and disturbs their nests.

Supporting Details

Unstated Main Idea

Overview Summarizing Fiction

Directions and Sample Answers for Activity Pages

Day 1	See "Provide a Real-World Example" below.
Day 2	Read and discuss the story. Then ask students to draw a circle around the best answers. (**Big Ideas:** Elizabeth and Jacob find a chest in the sand. The treasure in the chest is rocks. **Summary:** Two kids find a treasure chest full of rocks at a beach.)
Day 3	Read and discuss the story. Then ask students to underline the big ideas and write a summary. (**Big Ideas:** I'm practicing for a bubble gum-blowing contest I entered. I'm tired of watching you. I'm tired of that popping sound. Patrick won first place. The prize is a five-pound bag of bubble gum. Oh, no! **Summary:** Patrick's family is tired of his bubble-blowing, so they're not pleased when he wins a large bag of bubble gum in a contest.)
Day 4	Read and discuss the story. Then ask students to cross out the sentences that don't belong. (**Big Ideas:** Cross out "Long ago, cats and dogs were friends" and "Cat plays with his friends all day." **Summary:** Cross out "Dog hides in Cat's house to see if Cat is sick" and "Dog cooks dinner when Cat is sick.")
Day 5	Read the story together. Ask students to record the big ideas and a summary on their graphic organizers. Afterward, meet individually with students to discuss their results. Use their responses to plan further instruction and review. (**Big Ideas:** Dragonfly flaps his wings at Bumblebee. Dragonfly says he'll eat Firefly. Dragonfly chases Butterfly. None of them get upset. **Summary:** Dragonfly tries to be mean like a dragon, but his friends know he's nice.)

Provide a Real-World Example

◆ Hand out the Day 1 activity page.

◆ **Say:** *A boy went to a carnival. He rode the roller coaster and spinner. Then he tossed beanbags through holes and threw balls in buckets. Let's think about the big ideas. A boy went to a . . .* (**carnival**). *He went on some . . .* (**rides**). *He played some . . .* (**games**). Allow time for students to record these activities under **Big Ideas.**

◆ **Say:** *I can summarize the boy's day in one sentence: A boy went on rides and played games at a carnival.* Allow time for students to complete the summary.

◆ **Say:** *A girl went to a sea aquarium. She saw beautiful plants in the water. She saw sharks in tanks. Then she watched a dolphin show.*

◆ Ask students to record the big ideas (**sea aquarium, plants, sharks/dolphins**) and compose a summary, such as: A girl saw plants and animals at a sea aquarium.

◆ Explain that students can also summarize stories they read. Write the following on chart paper:

Summarizing Fiction

Think about what you read.

Pick out the big ideas.

Write one or two sentences about the big ideas.

Name _____

Places to Go

Listen to the story. Then write the big ideas. Then complete the summary.

Big Ideas:

A boy went to a _____.

He went on some _____.

He played some _____.

Summary:

A boy went on _____ and played _____ at a _____.

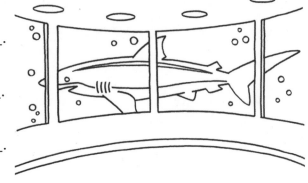

Big Ideas:

A girl went to a _____.

She saw _____.

She saw _____ and _____.

Summary:

_____

_____

The Treasure Chest

Read the story. Then draw a circle around the best answers.

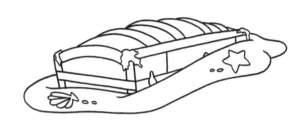

Jacob and Elizabeth ambled down the beach, squishing wet sand between their toes. "Look at the tide pools!" said Jacob. "Look at the clumps of seaweed!"

When they came to the bend in the cove, Elizabeth spotted something half-buried in the sand. "It's a treasure chest!" she exclaimed.

Jacob and Elizabeth ran to the chest and tried to pull it out, but it wouldn't budge. Shoveling sand with their hands, they uncovered a handle on one end and soon tugged the heavy chest out of the sand.

"It's not locked," said Jacob. S-l-o-w-l-y Elizabeth lifted the lid. Had she found gold? Money? Jewels?

"It's rocks!" Jacob cried. "Oh, well . . . at least we can say we have our very own treasure chest!"

What are the story's big ideas?

Jacob likes to examine tide pools and clumps of seaweed.

The kids like to squish wet sand between their toes.

The cove of the beach has a bend.

Elizabeth and Jacob find a chest in the sand.

The chest has a handle on one end.

The treasure in the chest is rocks.

Which sentence best summarizes the story?

Two kids see tide pools and seaweed at a beach.

Two kids find a treasure chest full of rocks at a beach.

Two kids figure out how to dig a chest out of sand.

Name _____

Big Bubbles

**Read the story. Draw a line under the big ideas.
Then write a summary.**

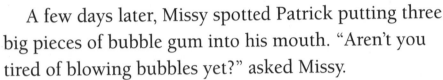

"Hey, Patrick—what're you doing?" asked Missy.

"I'm practicing for a bubble gum-blowing contest
I entered," said Patrick. "I'm going to keep practicing
every day after school. Then I'll practice again after
dinner."

A few days later, Missy spotted Patrick putting three
big pieces of bubble gum into his mouth. "Aren't you
tired of blowing bubbles yet?" asked Missy.

"I know I'm tired of watching you," said their older brother Quenton.
"Besides that, no one can understand what you're saying when your mouth
is stuffed with gum."

"And I'm tired of that popping sound!" said Mom. "I'll be glad when this contest
is over."

The day of the contest arrived, and Patrick won first place. "Yeah!" he cried.

"The prize is a five-pound bag of bubble gum!" said the judge.

"Oh, no!" said Missy, Quenton, and Mom.

Summary: _____

_____

_____

Unit 11 • *Everyday Comprehension Intervention Activities Grade 4* • ©2010 Newmark Learning, LLC

Why Dogs Chase Cats

Read the story. In the first box, cross out the sentences that are not big ideas.
In the second box, cross out the sentences that are not the best summary.

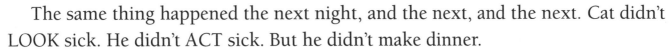

Long ago, dogs and cats were friends. "I'll work all day and earn money for food," said Dog.

"And I'll cook the food," said Cat. Every night, Dog went to Cat's house for dinner. Then, one night, no dinner was on the table. "I don't feel well," said Cat.

"OK," said Dog. "I'll make my own dinner tonight. Take care!"

The same thing happened the next night, and the next, and the next. Cat didn't LOOK sick. He didn't ACT sick. But he didn't make dinner.

One morning, Dog stayed home from work and hid in Cat's house. Cat played with his friends all day long. At dinner time, Dog jumped out from behind the sofa. "You lied!" he said. "You're not sick!" He chased Cat all around the house. And that is why dogs still chase cats today.

Big Ideas	**Summary**
Cat says he will cook dinner for Dog.	Dog hides in Cat's house to see if Cat is sick.
Long ago, cats and dogs were friends.	Dog finds out that Cat lied, so he chases Cat.
Dog is angry and chases Cat.	Dog cooks dinner when Cat is sick.
Cat plays with his friends all day.	
Cat lies to Dog about being sick.	
Dog works all day to earn money for food.	

Assessment

**Read the story. Then write the big ideas
and a summary in the boxes.**

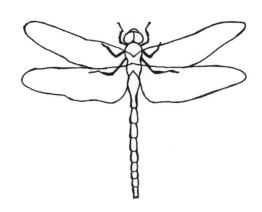

"I'm called a dragonfly," said Dragonfly. "So why can't I be ferocious and scary like a dragon?"

"Because you're nice," replied the other insects.

Dragonfly thought about what his friends had said. "Starting tomorrow, I'm going to be mean," he decided.

The next morning, Dragonfly flapped his wings in Bumblebee's face.

"That tickles!" said Bumblebee, buzzing a happy tune.

Discouraged, Dragonfly found Firefly. "I'm going to eat you!" he said.

But Firefly just laughed. "That's a funny joke," she said, glowing.

Finally, Dragonfly found Butterfly and chased her across the water.

"That was fun! Let's race again tomorrow!" said Butterfly, floating gently away.

Dragonfly sighed. "Maybe I should change my name to Goodfly," he said.

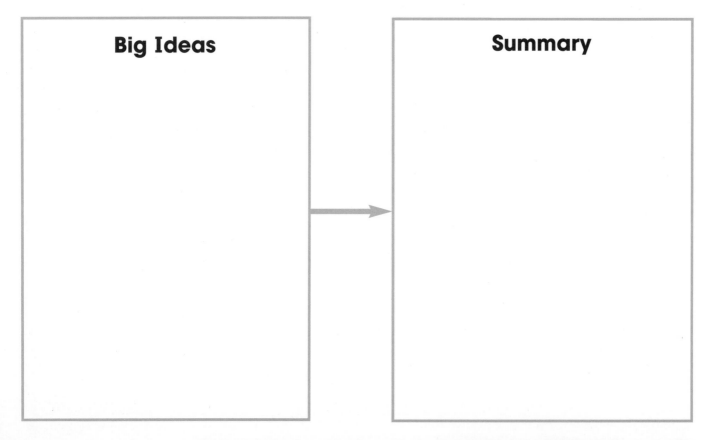

Big Ideas	Summary

Overview   Summarizing Nonfiction

Directions and Sample Answers for Activity Pages

Day 1	See "Provide a Real-World Example" below.
Day 2	Read and discuss the passage. Then ask students to draw a circle around the best answers. (**Big Ideas:** Hares and rabbits are different animals. The bodies and ears of hares and rabbits differ. **Summary:** Hares and rabbits are different animals with different bodies and ears.)
Day 3	Read and discuss the passage. Then ask students to fill in the blanks to complete the sentences. (**Big Ideas:** Pebble Patterns is a Native American game. The first player creates a pattern with pebbles. The other player tries to remake the pattern. **Summary:** Pebble Patterns is a Native American game in which a player tries to remake a pattern that another player created.)
Day 4	Read and discuss the passage. Then ask students to cross out the sentences that don't belong. (**Big Ideas:** Cross out "A seismograph measures seismic waves," "Some scientists study earthquakes," "Rocks inside Earth can break apart," and "Seismograph recordings are valuable." **Summary:** Cross out "There are two types of seismic waves" and "Scientists get information from a seismograph.")
Day 5	Read the passage together. Ask students to record the big ideas and a summary on their graphic organizers. Afterward, meet individually with students to discuss their results. Use their responses to plan further instruction and review. (**Big Ideas:** Toothed whales have teeth. They are hunters. Baleen whales have baleen plates. Baleen whales filter food from the water. **Summary:** Toothed whales hunt for food, but baleen whales filter food through baleen plates.)

Provide a Real-World Example

◆ Hand out the Day 1 activity page.

◆ **Say:** *A friend visited the Arizona-Sonora Desert Museum. The museum has desert animals. My friend saw mountain lions, leafcutter ants, and Gila monsters. Think about the big ideas. Put a check mark beside each big idea on the page.* (**many kinds of animals, Arizona-Sonora Desert Museum, desert animals**)

◆ **Say:** *I can summarize this information in one sentence: The Arizona-Sonora Desert Museum has many kinds of desert animals.* Allow time for students to complete the summary.

◆ **Say:** *At the museum, my friend learned that the Gila monster is the largest lizard in the United States. Some Gila monsters are two feet long. The Gila monster is also poisonous.*

◆ Ask students to put a check mark beside each big idea (**poisonous, largest lizard in United States, Gila monster**) and compose a summary, such as: The poisonous Gila monster is the largest lizard in the United States.

◆ Explain that students can also summarize when they read. Write the following on chart paper:

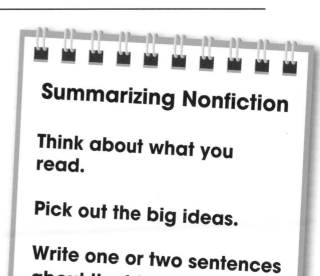

Summarizing Nonfiction

Think about what you read.

Pick out the big ideas.

Write one or two sentences about the big ideas.

Museum in the Desert

Listen to the example. Put a check mark next to each big idea. Then write a summary.

Big Ideas:

❏ many kinds of animals

❏ a friend

❏ Arizona-Sonora Desert Museum

❏ desert animals

❏ visiting a museum

Summary:

The _____ has many kinds of _____.

Big Ideas:

❏ poisonous

❏ two feet long

❏ museum

❏ largest lizard in United States

❏ Gila monster

Summary:

_____

_____

Long-Eared Critters

Read the passage. Then draw a circle around the best answers.

Many people think a hare and a rabbit are the same animal, but they are really quite different. A hare has an arched, streamlined body for running. A rabbit's body is rounder. A hare's ears are quite long and are always up. A rabbit has long ears, too, but some have "lop ears" that hang down. The names of some hares and rabbits are even more confusing. For example, a jackrabbit is really a hare, and a Belgian hare is really a rabbit!

What are the big ideas?
Hares and rabbits are different animals.
A streamlined body is good for running.
Ears that hang down are called lop ears.
The names of some rabbits and hares are confusing.
The bodies and ears of hares and rabbits differ.
The Belgian hare is a rabbit, not a hare.

Which sentence best summarizes the passage?
Both hares and rabbits have long ears.
Hares and rabbits are different animals with different
    bodies and ears.
People can tell a rabbit by its round body.

Pebble Patterns

Read the passage. Then complete the sentences.

Native Americans taught their children to pay careful attention to their surroundings in order to stay safe. One way children developed this skill was by playing a game called Pebble Patterns. First, the players collected 30 pebbles of different sizes and colors. The first player created a pattern with some of the pebbles. The other player studied the pattern for a certain amount of time. When the time limit was up, the first player destroyed the pattern, and the other player tried to remake it. Players could make the game more challenging by using more pebbles and creating more complex patterns.

Big Ideas:

Pebble Patterns is a _____ game.

The first player _____ with pebbles.

The other player tries to _____ .

Summary:

Pebble Patterns is a _____ in which

a player tries to _____ that

another player created.

Unit 12 • Everyday Comprehension Intervention Activities Grade 4 • ©2010 Newmark Learning, LLC

Name _____

Seismic Waves

Read the passage. In the first box, cross out the sentences that are not big ideas. In the second box, cross out the sentences that are not the best summary.

Rock inside Earth may suddenly break apart. Then, the ground moves, creating an earthquake. Earthquakes produce energy. The energy comes in the form of seismic waves. The two types of seismic waves are body waves and surface waves. Body waves move through the inner layers of Earth. Surface waves travel along the crust, or surface, of Earth.

Body waves occur before surface waves, but surface waves are the ones that damage land and buildings. An instrument called a seismograph measures and records seismic waves. These recordings are extremely valuable to scientists who study earthquakes.

Big Ideas	**Summary**
A seismograph measures seismic waves.	There are two types of seismic waves.
Seismic waves are waves of energy.	Scientists get information from a seismograph.
Some scientists study earthquakes.	Earthquakes produce waves of energy called seismic waves.
Earthquakes produce energy.	
Rocks inside Earth can break apart.	
Seismograph recordings are valuable.	

Assessment

Read the passage. Then write the big ideas and a summary in the boxes.

Not all whales eat the same way. Whales with teeth, called toothed whales, are hunters. They chase sea creatures such as fish, crabs, shrimp, or squid and swallow them whole. Other whales have baleen plates instead of teeth. Baleen is a strong, stiff material with hairy edges that hangs from the top of the whale's mouth. A baleen whale feeds by filling its mouth with water and filtering the water through its plates. The whale then swallows the small fish and tiny shrimp-like animals (krill) that the water leaves in its mouth.

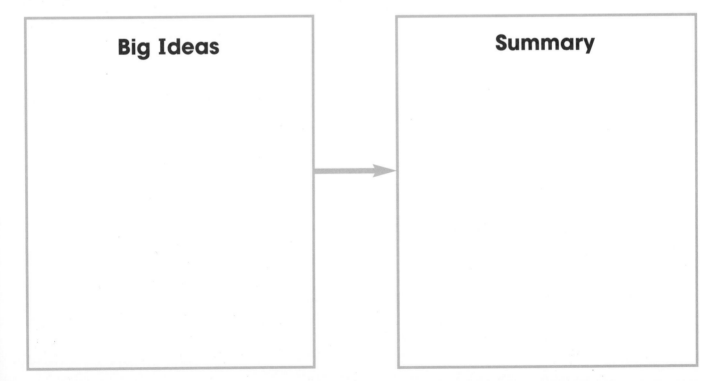

Big Ideas

Summary

Overview Comparing and Contrasting in Fiction

Directions and Sample Answers for Activity Pages

Day 1	See "Provide a Real-World Example" below.
Day 2	Read and discuss the story. Ask students to underline the compare and contrast signal words in the story. Then ask them to fill in the Venn diagram. (**Signal Words: both, however, different, on the other hand, in common, same, alike, both. Juan:** Bullfrog team, forward. **Both:** play soccer, have jersey number 00, love ice cream. **David:** Hornet team, goalie)
Day 3	Read and discuss the story. Ask students to mark the chart by placing Xs in the appropriate columns to show how Pepper and Shadow are alike and different. Then ask them to add one more detail to compare and contrast. (**Pepper:** uses the little door, short tail, runs fast, friendly, plays with yarn. **Shadow:** uses the little door, long tail, runs fast, shy, naps on beds, plays with yarn)
Day 4	Read and discuss the story. Then ask students to mark each statement true or false and to correct any false statements. (**1:** False. Crabby is cross. **2:** False. Jolly is pleasant. **3:** True. **4:** True. **5:** True. **6:** False. Jolly smiles at the forest animals. **7:** False. Crabby scares the forest animals.)
Day 5	Read the story together. Ask students to fill in the chart to compare and contrast Maria and Nora. Afterward, meet individually with students to discuss their results. Use their responses to plan further instruction and review. (**Maria:** draws with colored chalk, draws people, making a collage. **Maria and Nora:** favorite subject is art, have sketchbooks, will be in art show. **Nora:** draws with colored pencils, draws animals, making clay animals)

Provide a Real-World Example

◆ Hand out the Day 1 activity page.

◆ **Say:** *I will say some phrases. If a phrase describes you, stand up. If not, remain seated.* Call out phrases such as *have a dog, like pickles, enjoy soccer,* and *have blue eyes.*

◆ Explain that discovering ways classmates are alike is comparing. Discovering ways they are different is contrasting.

◆ Invite volunteers to create oral sentences comparing or contrasting themselves to classmates. Write signal words they use on the board, such as *Lizzie and I* **both** *have dogs. Billy likes pickles, and I like pickles,* **too**. *Kris enjoys soccer,* **but** *I don't. My eyes are a* **different** *color than Robert's.*

◆ Give student pairs a few minutes to interview each other and fill in the sentences on their pages. Invite them to share their findings.

◆ Explain that they can also compare and contrast when they read stories. Write the following on chart paper:

Comparing and Contrasting in Fiction

Find things in a story that are alike.

Look for compare signal words like *too, both, alike, same,* and *in common*.

Find things in the story that are different.

Look for contrast signal words like *different, but, however,* and *on the other hand*.

Alike and Different

How are you and your partner alike? How are you and your partner different?

Comparing

_____and I **both** have _____.

I like _____, and _____ likes

_____, **too**.

Contrasting

_____ and I have **different** _____.

_____ likes _____, **but** I like

_____.

Soccer on Saturdays

Read the story. Draw a line under the compare-and-contrast signal words. Then fill in the Venn diagram.

Juan and David are best friends. They both have soccer practice on Saturdays. However, they don't see each other until practice is over, because they play on different teams.

"How's the Bullfrog team doing? C-r-o-a-k . . . c-r-o-a-k . . .," teased David.

"Fine! How's the Hornet team doing? Bzzz . . . . bzzz . . . .bzzz . . .," Juan teased back.

"I'm goalie this year," said David.

"Jumping, diving, and throwing the ball sound like fun," said Juan. "On the other hand, I like to score and show off my fancy foot moves, so I'm glad I'm a forward."

"We do have one thing in common," said David. "We have the same number on our jerseys this year—00!"

"I can think of another way we're alike," said Juan. "We both love ice cream. Let's go get some right now!"

Juan   **Both**   **David**

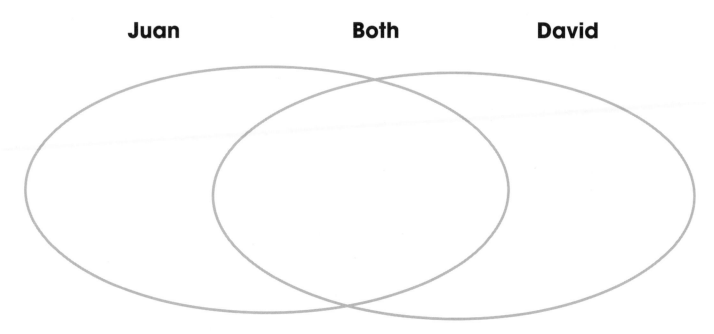

The Little Door

Read the story. Then mark the chart to compare and contrast Pepper and Shadow. At the bottom of the chart, add one more detail to compare and contrast.

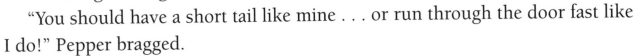

"I love this little door," said Pepper the cat. "I can go outside whenever I want to."

"I like it, too," said Shadow. "But my long tail sometimes gets caught, and that HURTS!"

"You should have a short tail like mine . . . or run through the door fast like I do!" Pepper bragged.

"I do run fast when I see a human," said Shadow.

"You should play with the humans like I do," said Pepper.

"I like to sneak in the humans' rooms and nap on their beds," said Shadow. "But speaking of playing, where's our ball of yarn?"

"Here it is," said Pepper. "Catch!"

	Pepper	**Shadow**
uses the little door		
long tail		
short tail		
runs fast		
shy		
friendly		
naps on beds		
plays with yarn		

Crabby and Jolly

Read the story. Then mark each statement true (T) or false (F). If the statement is false, write a true statement on the line.

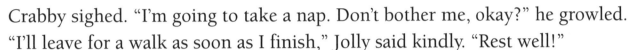

In the hollow of an ancient oak tree live two elves. "I HATE having dirt on the floor," said Crabby, scowling at some dust the wind blew in.

"Me, too," said Jolly, humming a cheerful tune as he danced around the floor with the broom.

Crabby sighed. "I'm going to take a nap. Don't bother me, okay?" he growled.

"I'll leave for a walk as soon as I finish," Jolly said kindly. "Rest well!"

As Jolly walked, he was surprised to see all the forest animals running away. "What's wrong?" he wondered.

Suddenly, an owl swooped down and started laughing. "Don't be afraid, everyone . . . it's Jolly!"

The other animals soon gathered around Jolly. "We're sorry we ran away," they said. "You and Crabby both wear green pants and orange shirts. Luckily, Owl got close enough to see a smile, so he knew it was you!"

Crabby and Jolly . . .

1. _____ are both cross. _____

2. _____ are both pleasant. _____

3. _____ both like their tree hollow to be clean. _____

4. _____ dress alike. _____

5. _____ are hard to tell apart from a distance. _____

6. _____ both smile at the forest animals. _____

7. _____ both scare the forest animals. _____

Assessment

Read the story. Then fill in the chart to show how Maria and Nora are alike and different.

"I'm sure glad it's art day," said Maria. "Art is my favorite subject."

"Mine, too," said Nora. "I know you like to draw with colored chalk best, but I like to use colored pencils."

"Let's ask our parents if we can go to the park after school," suggested Maria. "We could take our sketchbooks."

"Good idea!" said Nora. "You like to draw people, and we'll see lots of people. On the other hand, I have to look a little harder for animals to draw. Did you know I'm also making some clay animals for the art show next month?"

"I'd love to see them!" said Maria. "I'm making a collage from my people drawings for the show."

"None of my clay animals looks like you," Nora teased. "But I hope one of your people drawings looks like me!"

Maria	Maria and Nora	Nora

Overview Comparing and Contrasting in Nonfiction

Directions and Sample Answers for Activity Pages

Day 1	See "Provide a Real-World Example" below.
Day 2	Read and discuss the passage. Ask students to underline the compare and contrast signal words in the passage. Then ask them to fill in the Venn diagram. (**Signal Words: both, whereas, however, while, also. Hurricane:** leave the area, starts over ocean, ring of clouds, may last a day or more. **Both:** powerful and dangerous storms, violent winds, can cause severe damage. **Tornado:** go to a basement or shelter, starts over land, funnel-shaped cloud, may come and go within an hour.)
Day 3	Read and discuss the passage. Then ask students to answer the questions. (**1:** Both are ports on one of the Great Lakes. **2:** Chicago is in the United States, but Toronto is in Canada. **3:** Toronto is the largest city in its province, and Chicago is the largest city in its state. **4:** Toronto is the capital of its province, but Chicago is not the capital of its state.)
Day 4	Read and discuss the passage. Then ask students to circle the best answers. (**1:** both. **2:** dolphin. **3:** swordfish. **4:** both. **5:** both. **6:** dolphin. **7:** swordfish. **8:** both. **9:** dolphin. **10:** swordfish. **11:** both. **12:** dolphin.)
Day 5	Read the passage together. Ask students to fill in the chart to compare and contrast the insects. Afterward, meet individually with students to discuss their results. Use their responses to plan further instruction and review. (**Ants:** have soldiers, eat small insects. **Ants and Honeybees:** live in a colony, have specific job to do, have a queen and workers. **Honeybees:** gather nectar and pollen for food, make honey, build a honeycomb.)

Provide a Real-World Example

◆ Hand out the Day 1 activity page.

◆ **Say:** *A few days ago, I looked at a lime and a grapefruit at the grocery store. I compared the two fruits by thinking of ways they are alike. I contrasted them by thinking of ways they are different. I noticed their sizes, shapes, and colors. I thought about their tastes.*

◆ Read the first sentence and ask students to circle the word **but**. **Say:** *But is a signal word we use to contrast two things.* Then ask students put a check mark in the chart to show that the sizes of the fruits are different.

◆ Repeat the process with the other sentences, asking volunteers to identify the signal words. Point out that **different** and **while** signal contrasts, and **both** signals a comparison.

◆ Explain that students can also compare and contrast when they read. Write the following on chart paper:

> ## Comparing and Contrasting in Nonfiction
> **Find things in a passage that are alike.**
>
> **Look for compare signal words like** *too, both, also, alike, similar,* **and** *in common.*
>
> **Find things in the passage that are different.**
>
> **Look for contrast signal words like** *but, whereas, however, while, different,* **and** *unlike.*

Fruit

Read the passage. Circle compare and contrast signal words. Then use the chart to compare and contrast limes and grapefruits.

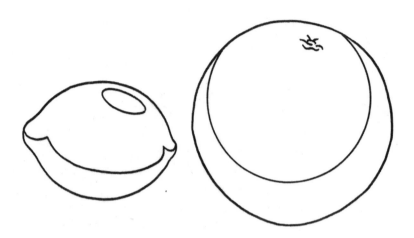

A lime is a small fruit, but a grapefruit is big.

Limes and grapefruits are different shapes.

A lime is green, while a grapefruit is yellow.

Limes and grapefruits both taste sour.

	Same	**Different**
size		
shape		
color		
taste		

Wild Winds

**Read the passage. Draw a line under the compare-and-contrast signal words.
Then fill in the Venn diagram.**

Warning! The hurricane will hit land within hours. Be prepared to leave the area. **Warning!** Trackers have spotted a tornado. Go to a basement or shelter immediately. Both hurricanes and tornadoes are powerful, dangerous storms that produce violent winds. A hurricane starts over the ocean and often moves toward land, whereas a tornado starts over land. The swirling winds of a hurricane form a ring of clouds. However, a tornado's winds spin into a dark, funnel-shaped cloud.

While a hurricane may last a day or more, a tornado may come and go within an hour. Hurricanes can cause severe damage, crushing everything from homes and office buildings to cars and trees. Tornadoes can also cause severe damage, destroying everything in their way.

Hurricane   **Both**   **Tornado**

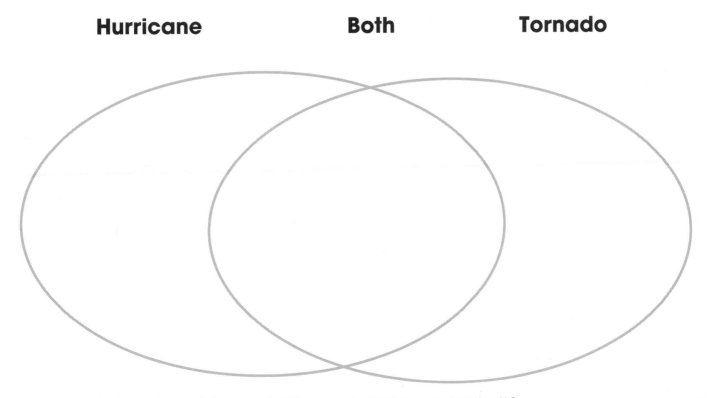

Two Large Cities

Read the passage. Then answer the questions.

Waves and skylines meet in the downtown sections of two large cities—Chicago and Toronto. Chicago sits on the shore of one of the Great Lakes, Lake Michigan. Toronto also sits on a Great Lake, Lake Ontario. With their large bodies of water, both cities are ports. Chicago is on the United States side of the Great Lakes, while Toronto is on Canada's side. Toronto is the largest city and the capital of the province of Ontario. Chicago is the largest city in Illinois, but it is not the capital of the state.

1. How are the locations of the cities similar?

_____

2. How are the locations of the cities different?

_____

3. How else are the two cities alike?

_____

4. How else are the two cities different?

_____

Unit 14 • Everyday Comprehension Intervention Activities Grade 4 • ©2010 Newmark Learning, LLC

Sea Animals

**Read the passage. Then circle
the correct word for each description.**

Dolphins and swordfish are both creatures of the sea. Swordfish are a large type of fish. Dolphins are also large. Unlike swordfish, dolphins are mammals. Dolphins like shallow water, and swordfish do, too. The two animals have speed in common. Dolphins swim fast, and swordfish swim even faster. While several dolphins often swim together in schools, swordfish prefer to be alone. Both animals have the same streamlined body shape. However, their heads are not at all alike. A dolphin has a smooth head, but a swordfish has a long sword-like bill sticking out from its upper jaw. Both creatures frequently leap from the sea, but only the dolphin makes sounds.

1. sea creature	dolphin	swordfish	both
2. mammal	dolphin	swordfish	both
3. fish	dolphin	swordfish	both
4. likes shallow water	dolphin	swordfish	both
5. fast swimmer	dolphin	swordfish	both
6. swims in schools	dolphin	swordfish	both
7. swims alone	dolphin	swordfish	both
8. streamlined body	dolphin	swordfish	both
9. smooth head	dolphin	swordfish	both
10. sword on head	dolphin	swordfish	both
11. leaps from the sea	dolphin	swordfish	both
12. makes sounds	dolphin	swordfish	both

Assessment

Read the paragraph. Then fill in the chart to show how ants and honeybees are alike and different.

If you were an ant or a honeybee, you would live in a colony with your fellow insects. You would also have a specific job to do. The most important member of an ant colony is the queen. The queen has worker ants to take care of her and the nest, and soldier ants to protect the colony. A honeybee hive has a queen and workers, too. Ants eat small insects, while honeybees gather nectar and pollen for food. Honeybees use nectar to make honey. They store the honey in a honeycomb they build.

Ants	Ants and Honeybees	Honeybees

Overview Identifying Cause and Effect in Fiction

Directions and Sample Answers for Activity Pages

Day 1	See "Provide a Real-World Example" below.
Day 2	Read and discuss the story. Then ask students to underline the cause-and-effect signal words and answer the questions. (**Signal Words: because, if, therefore, since, so, as a result, why. 1:** The icy wind caused Man to shiver. **2:** Coyote is warm. **3:** He wanted to help. **4:** Coyote was able to grab a burning log. **5:** She saw Coyote stealing the fire. **6:** A Fire Being touched the tip with her fiery fingers.)
Day 3	Read and discuss the story. Then ask students to fill in the missing causes and effects. (**1:** She and Meg went to the pond. **2:** The pond had thin ice. **3:** She held Angela's hand. **4:** Angela was skating too fast. **5:** She learned to glide, twist, and spin like a skating star.)
Day 4	Read and discuss the story. Then ask students to fill in the cause-and-effect chain. (**2nd link:** Paul went to the kitchen to make breakfast. **4th link:** He looked for something to wipe up the mess. **6th link:** He grabbed the roll. **8th link:** The juice spilled off the counter.)
Day 5	Read the story together. Ask students to record three causes and effects on their graphic organizers. Afterward, meet individually with students to discuss their results. Use their responses to plan further instruction and review. (**Cause:** Elena ate a bag of candy. **Effect:** She felt sick. **Cause:** Elena's stomach hurt worse. **Effect:** She moaned, and Mom came running. **Cause:** Elena felt guilty. **Effect:** She started to cry. **Cause:** Mom was worried about Elena's crying. **Effect:** She called the doctor. **Cause:** The doctor wanted to see Elena. **Effect:** Mom made an appointment. **Cause:** Elena knew she wasn't really sick. **Effect:** She told Mom about the candy.)

Provide a Real-World Example

◆ Hand out the Day 1 activity page.

◆ Invite volunteers to role-play a situation in which the wind blows a spelling list out of their hand. After each example, ask classmates to state the cause, or reason, and the effect, or what happened. Encourage them to use cause-and-effect signal words, such as "The wind blew Tori's paper out of her hand, **so** she caught it and put it in her backpack" or "Pedro ran back to the classroom **because** the wind blew his spelling list away." Allow time for students to write or draw one of the effects in the top box on the page. Then ask them to write the words **cause** and **effect** under the appropriate boxes.

◆ Repeat the process with two additional school scenarios. (I forgot to bring my lunch to school. I got an overdue notice from the school library.)

◆ Explain that students can also identify cause-and-effect relationships when they read stories. Write the following on chart paper:

Identifying Cause and Effect in Fiction

Think about what made something happen. What was the cause, or reason?

Think about what happened. What was the effect, or result?

Look for cause-and-effect signal words like *because, since, therefore, so, why, if,* and *as a result.*

A Day at School

Look at each picture. Draw what happened next. Then label each cause and effect.

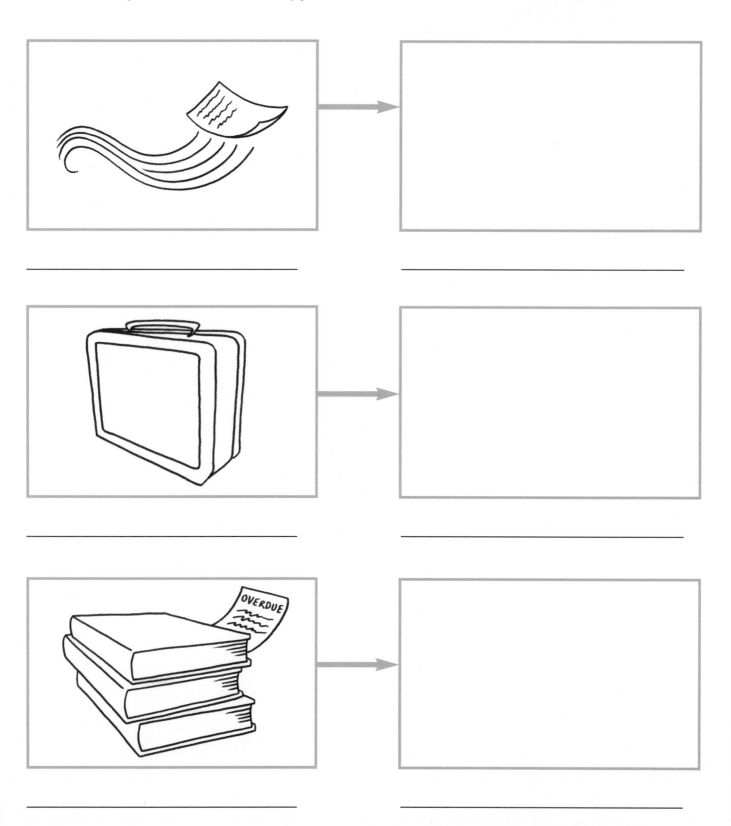

_____   _____

_____   _____

White-Tipped Tail

Read the story. Draw a line under the cause-and-effect signal words. Then answer the questions.

"I'm so cold," Man said to Coyote, shivering because of the icy wind. "If I had a fur coat like yours, I'd be warm."

"I want to help. Therefore, I plan to steal some fire from the Fire Beings," said Coyote.

"But they guard the fire day and night," said Man.

"I'll try to catch them as they change guards," said Coyote. "Wish me luck!"

Coyote went to the Fire Beings' cave and waited until they changed guards. Since one of the guards was slow to take her turn, Coyote was able to grab a flaming log. But suddenly, the guard saw Coyote. "He's stealing our fire, so I must leave my post!" called the guard.

Coyote got away, but not before the guard touched the tip of his tail with her fiery fingers. As a result, the tip turned white, and that is why coyotes still have white-tipped tails today.

1. What caused Man to shiver? _____

_____

2. What is the effect of Coyote's fur coat? _____

_____

3. Why did Coyote want to give fire to Man? _____

_____

4. What happened because the new guard was slow? _____

_____

5. What caused the guard to leave her post? _____

_____

6. Why did the tip of Coyote's tail turn white? _____

_____

Skating Star

Read the story. Then fill in the missing causes and effects.

Angela called Meg. "I got ice skates for my birthday, so let's go to the pond!"

The girls saw a sign at the pond: *Thin Ice!*

"We musn't take a chance," said Meg. "Let's go to the ice rink instead."

At the ice rink, Angela stepped onto the ice and immediately slipped and fell. After Meg helped Angela up, she continued holding her hand so her friend could get her balance. Soon, Angela was soaring across the ice on her own.

Then . . . crash! Angela fell again. "It's because I was skating too fast," she said, rubbing her leg. "I need more practice."

After that, Angela practiced every day. As a result, she learned to glide, twist, and spin like a skating star.

1. **Cause: Angela got ice skates.**
   Effect: _____

2. **Cause:** _____
   Effect: The girls went to the ice rink.

3. **Cause: Meg wanted to help her friend get her balance.**
   Effect: _____

4. **Cause:** _____
   Effect: Angela fell again.

5. **Cause: Angela practiced every day.**
   Effect: _____

Happy Father's Day, Dad!

**Sometimes an effect becomes the cause for the next effect.
Read the story. Then fill in the cause-and-effect chain.**

"Since it's Father's Day, I'm making you breakfast,"
Paul told Dad. He headed for the kitchen.

"Oops!" Paul said as he dropped a raw egg on the floor. He looked for something
to wipe up the mess. He spotted the paper towel roll on the counter. As he grabbed
it, he knocked over the glass of orange juice he had just poured. He watched as the
juice spilled off the counter and joined the gooey egg on the floor.

Paul went into the living room. "Dad, how about if I treat you to breakfast at the
corner diner?" he asked.

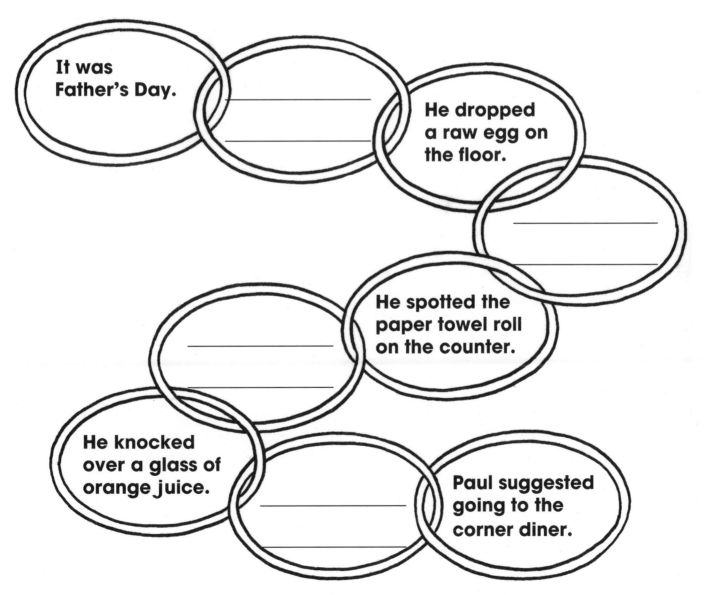

It was Father's Day.

_____

He dropped a raw egg on the floor.

_____

He spotted the paper towel roll on the counter.

_____

He knocked over a glass of orange juice.

_____

Paul suggested going to the corner diner.

Assessment

Read the story. Then fill in the graphic organizers to show three of the cause-and-effect relationships.

Elena ate a bag of candy. "Oh . . . I feel sick!" Elena thought to herself. "I can't tell Mom. She'd be really upset."

Soon, Elena's stomach hurt even worse. She moaned, and Mom came running. "Poor thing!" said Mom. "Maybe some toast would help."

Feeling guilty, Elena started to cry. "Now I'm really worried," said Mom. "You must have the flu. I'll call the doctor." She went to the phone. "Dr. Mars wants to see you, so I made an appointment for 2:00."

Elena had no choice now. "It's my fault, Mom," she whimpered. "I ate a whole bag of candy!"

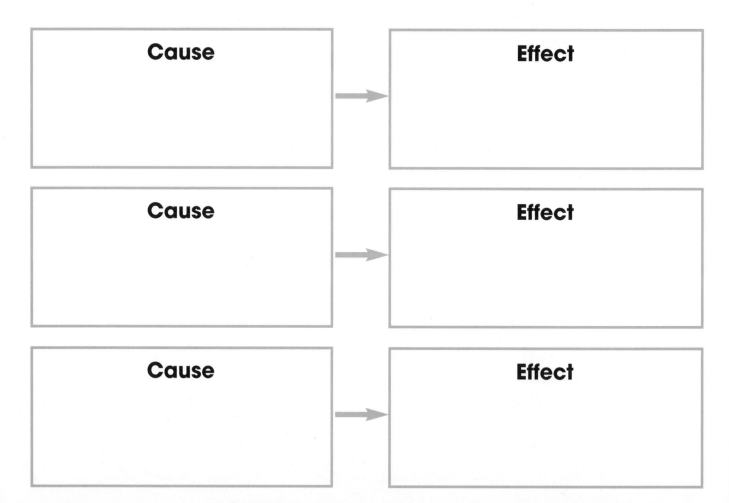

Cause		Effect
	→	
Cause		**Effect**
	→	
Cause		**Effect**
	→	

Overview Identifying Cause and Effect in Nonfiction

Directions and Sample Answers for Activity Pages

Day 1	See "Provide a Real-World Example" below.
Day 2	Read and discuss the passage. Then ask students to underline the cause-and-effect signal words and answer the questions. (**Signal Words: because, therefore, since, so, as a result. 1:** People need the water for themselves. **2:** There is less water. **3:** The water birds have less food. **4:** Some wetlands are almost dry.)
Day 3	Read and discuss the passage. Then ask students to write an effect for each cause. (**1:** They watched pigeons fly. **2:** They could turn in the air. **3:** They could test their glider. **4:** They flew the glider like a kite.)
Day 4	Read and discuss the passage. Then ask students to fill in the missing causes and effects. (**1:** It doesn't topple from the strong desert winds. **2:** The stems can expand to store water. **3:** It's a good food source for desert animals. **4:** Desert birds peck small holes in the saguaro's trunk.)
Day 5	Read the passage together. Ask students to record three causes and effects on their graphic organizers. Afterward, meet individually with students to discuss their results. Use their responses to plan further instruction and review. (**Cause:** All the parts of your ear work together. **Effect:** You can hear. **Cause:** The outer ear is shaped like a cup. **Effect:** It collects sound waves easily. **Cause:** The sound waves travel to the middle ear. **Effect:** The eardrum moves back and forth. **Cause:** The sound waves move the eardrum. **Effect:** Small bones around the eardrum vibrate. **Cause:** Nerves in your cochlea change the vibrations into messages and send them to your brain. **Effect:** Message heard!)

Provide a Real-World Example

◆ Hand out the Day 1 activity page.

◆ Invite volunteers to role-play a situation in which someone has prepared well for a piano recital. After each example, ask classmates to state the cause, or reason, and the effect, or what happened. Encourage them to use cause-and-effect signal words, such as **Since** *I knew my piece, I wasn't very nervous* or *I played beautifully,* **so** *everyone clapped loudly.* Allow time for students to write or draw one of the effects in the top box on the page. Then ask them to write the words **cause** and **effect** under the appropriate boxes.

◆ Repeat the process with two additional scenarios. (I just found out my best friend broke her arm. My cat ran out the door as I was leaving to go swimming.)

◆ Explain that students can also identify cause-and-effect relationships when they read. Write the following on chart paper:

Identifying Cause and Effect in Nonfiction

Think about what made something happen. What was the cause, or reason?

Think about what happened. What was the effect, or result?

Look for cause-and-effect signal words like *because, since, therefore, so, if, in order for,* **and** *as a result.*

What Happened?

Look at each picture. Write or draw what happened next. Then label each *cause* or *effect*.

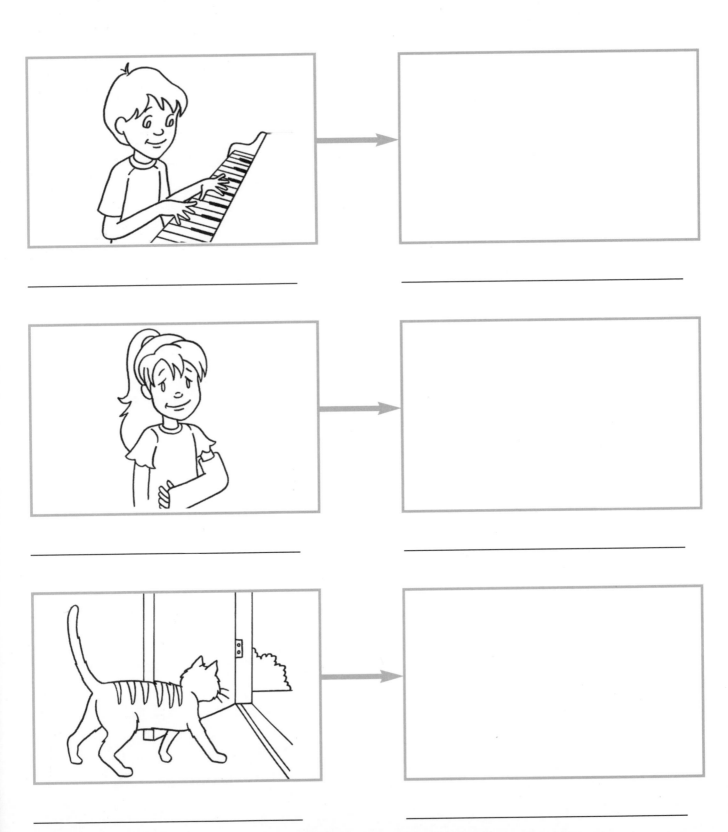

Dry Wetlands

Read the passage. Draw a line under the cause-and-effect signal words. Then answer the questions.

Many wild animals are losing their habitats because of people. For example, some wetland habitats are not as wet as they used to be. People who move to wetland areas need the water for themselves.

Therefore, there is less water for the animals. Since there is less water, there are fewer fish. The water birds that live in the wetlands eat fish, so they have less food. In some wetlands, people are using an enormous amount of water. As a result, these wetlands are almost dry.

1. Why do animals have less water in today's wetlands?

_____

2. Why do today's wetlands have fewer fish?

_____

3. What problem does having fewer fish cause?

_____

4. What happens as a result of people using an enormous amount of water?

_____

Flying Machine

Read the passage. Then write an effect for each cause.

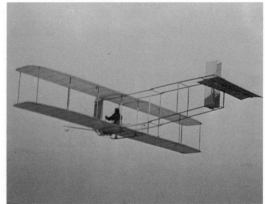

Two brothers, Orville and Wilbur Wright, were eager to build an aircraft. They wanted to know if wings could control an aircraft, so they watched pigeons fly. They noticed that the birds could turn in the air if they changed the positions of their wings. Orville and Wilbur used this information to build a glider. Then they traveled to a windy place in Kitty Hawk, North Carolina, so they could test their glider. The brothers realized that flying the glider with a pilot was dangerous. Therefore, they flew it like a kite with cords attached. After the test, the brothers eventually built a new aircraft with better wings, propellers, and an engine. This model, with one of the brothers as a pilot, stayed up for only a few seconds. But the brothers had built a true flying machine!

Cause	Effect
1. The brothers wanted to know if wings could control an aircraft.	_____ _____
2. The birds changed the positions of their wings.	_____ _____
3. The brothers found a windy place.	_____ _____
4. Flying the glider with a pilot was dangerous.	_____ _____

The Saguaro Cactus

Read the passage. Then fill in the missing causes and effects.

The saguaro cactus is a giant plant, standing up to fifty feet tall. The heavy saguaro doesn't topple from the strong desert winds because its roots wrap around rocks and anchor it. It has a thick trunk and several stems, or arms, that curve up. The stems can expand to store water. As a result, the plant can bloom without rain. The saguaro cactus also has fruit, making it a good food source for desert animals. Two desert birds, the Gila Woodpecker and the Gilded Flicker, peck small holes in the saguaro's trunk in order to make homes in it.

1. **Cause: The saguaro's roots wrap around rocks and anchor it.**
   Effect: _____

2. **Cause:** _____
   Effect: The saguaro can bloom without rain.

3. **Cause: The saguaro has fruit.**
   Effect: _____

4. **Cause:** _____
   Effect: The birds can make homes in the trunk.

Assessment

Read the passage. Then fill in the graphic organizers to show three cause-and-effect relationships.

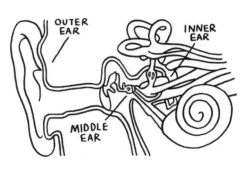

    Your ear has many parts, and all the parts must work together in order for you to hear. The three main parts are the outer ear, middle ear, and inner ear. The outer ear picks up sound waves from the air. Because the outer ear is shaped like a cup, it collects these sound waves easily. The sound waves then travel to the middle ear, causing the eardrum to move back and forth. As a result, small bones around the eardrum vibrate. These vibrations move into the inner ear where they meet a part called the cochlea. Nerves in your cochlea change the vibrations into messages and send them to your brain—message heard!

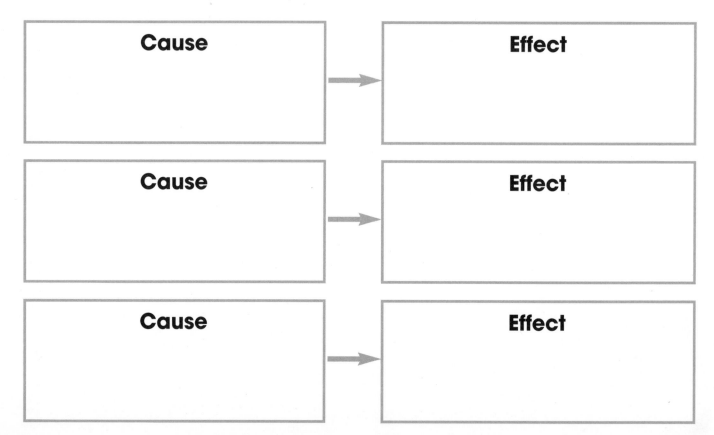

Unit 16 • Everyday Comprehension Intervention Activities Grade 4 • ©2010 Newmark Learning, LLC

Overview Making Inferences in Fiction

Directions and Sample Answers for Activity Pages

Day 1	See "Provide a Real-World Example" below.
Day 2	Read and discuss the story. Then ask students to color the circles in front of the best answers. (**1:** Mrs. Perez had lived at the farm since she was a young girl. Mrs. Ross saw little painted faces in the trunk. **2:** Many young girls play with dolls. **3:** Mrs. Ross found old dolls in the last trunk.)
Day 3	Read and discuss the story. Then ask students to answer the questions. (**1:** The animals laugh at Platypus. He quickly digs a hole to hide in. **2:** No one likes to be laughed at. **3:** Platypus is embarrassed by the way he looks.)
Day 4	Read and discuss the story. Then ask students to write their ideas in the boxes. (**Clues:** Lily loves to pick out her own clothes. Mom surveys Lily's outfit carefully. **Already Know:** Some parents don't approve of the way their children dress. **Inference:** Mom likes to check out Lily's outfits before she leaves the house.)
Day 5	Read the story together. Ask students to record clues, prior knowledge, and an inference. Afterward, meet individually with students to discuss their results. Use their responses to plan further instruction and review. (**Clues:** Brian groaned when he saw his hair cut short. He grew his curls out again. **Prior Knowledge:** Most people like to wear their hair a certain way. **Inference:** Brian likes his hair best when it's curly.)

Provide a Real-World Example

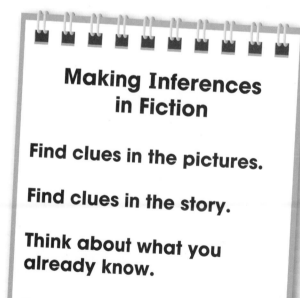

Making Inferences in Fiction

Find clues in the pictures.

Find clues in the story.

Think about what you already know.

Try to figure out what the author does not state.

◆ On cards, write sports scenarios for students to pantomime, such as "You just scored the winning point in the basketball game" or "The coach just called to say your soccer game was rained out." Hand out the Day 1 activity page.

◆ Invite students to take turns acting out a scenario without speaking while classmates try to figure out what is happening. **Say:** *Use the actor's clues along with your own prior knowledge to figure out, or infer, what situation the actor is pantomiming.*

◆ After each pantomime, discuss students' inferences. **Ask:** *What clues did the actor give? What prior knowledge did you use to help make the inference?* Point out that an inference, while logical, may not always be correct.

◆ Ask students to study the clues in the vacation drawings on the page and use their prior knowledge to write an inference for each one. Allow time for students to share and compare their results.

◆ Explain that they can also make inferences when they read stories. Write the following on chart paper:

Vacation Time

Study each picture. Look for clues. Then make an inference.

Inference

_____

_____

_____

_____

_____

Inference

_____

_____

_____

_____

_____

Seven Trunks

Read the story. Then read the questions and color the circles in front of the best answers.

"I just bought a farm. I love it here!" Mrs. Ross told her cousin on the phone. "Mrs. Perez lived here for more than seventy years—ever since she was a young girl. She said she left some things in the barn. I plan to go check it out today!"

Once her eyes adjusted to the barn's darkness, Mrs. Ross saw seven old trunks lined up in the corner. "What have we here?" Mrs. Ross asked herself.

All the trunks were locked. After finding some old tools to use to break the lock, Mrs. Ross opened the first trunk. Empty! "Well, that's disappointing!" she said. One by one, she opened each trunk. Empty, empty, empty, empty, and empty. "One more chance," Mrs. Ross said. With a mighty smack, she broke the last lock. When she opened the lid, dozens of little painted faces peered out.

1. Which clues are in the story?

O Mrs. Perez had lived at the farm since she was a young girl.

O Mrs. Perez played with dolls as a child.

O Mrs. Ross saw little painted faces in the trunk.

2. What do you already know?

O Many young girls play with dolls.

O Old trunks often have dolls in them.

O Old barns often have trunks in them.

3. Which is the best inference?

O Mrs. Ross found old blankets in the last trunk.

O Mrs. Ross found old dolls in the last trunk.

O Mrs. Ross found old clothes in the last trunk.

A New Look

Read the story. Then answer each question.

"Hi, Goat!" said Earth.

"I'm not Goat, I'm Squirrel," said Squirrel.

"Oh, I do get so confused. All you animals look exactly alike," said Earth. "I know! I'll have a party and give everyone something special! Tell all the animals to gather here tomorrow afternoon."

Platypus forgot about the party and went for a swim. "Where is everyone?" he wondered. Soon, a shiny creature approached him. "Hi, Platypus! It's Fish! Look at the beautiful scales I got at the party! You'd better hurry . . . it's almost over!"

"Oh, my!" said Earth when Platypus arrived. "All I have are a few leftover parts. Here's an extra beaver's tail, an extra duck's bill, and some extra bear's fur. Now, run along!"

When the other animals laughed at Platypus's new look, he quickly dug a hole. Platypuses still hide in holes to this very day.

1. What events are clues about how Platypus feels?

_____

_____

2. What do you already know?

_____

_____

3. What inference can you make about Platypus?

_____

_____

Camp Clothes

Read the story. Then write your ideas in the boxes.

"Thanks for taking me shopping, Mom!" Lily exclaimed. "I love picking out my own clothes."

"Let's see what you're wearing to camp today," Mom said. She surveyed Lily's outfit carefully. Jeans shorts. A T-shirt with a photo of Lily's favorite singers. A white sock with blue stars on it, and a blue sock with white stars on it. The names of the singers were written on her sneakers.

"Very . . . interesting," said Mom. "But I like it!"

"Oh . . . I forgot the best part!" Lily said. She ran to her room and came out in a straw hat with a big flower on one side, and sunglasses. "NOW I'm ready for camp," she said.

I know from the story that . . .

I already know . . .

I can infer that . . .

Assessment

Read the story. Then write the clues, your prior knowledge, and an inference in the boxes.

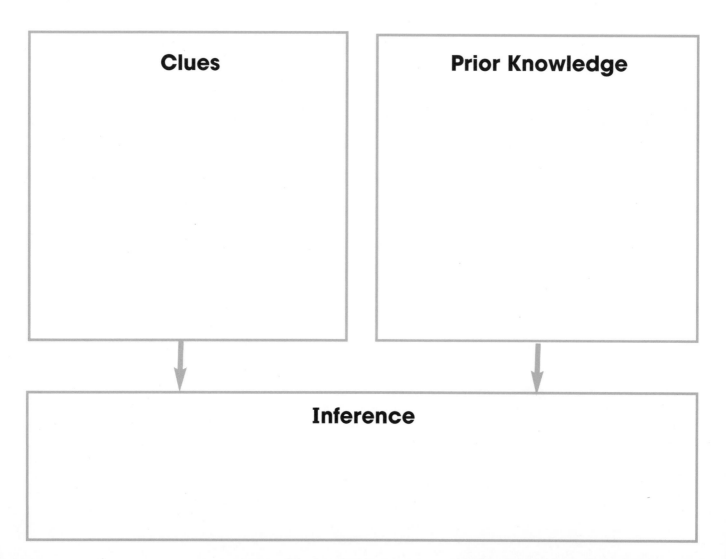

"Where are you going?" asked Marcus.

"To the barber shop," Brian replied. "I'm getting my hair cut really short."

"The barber will need garden shears to get through all those curls," teased Marcus.

After Brian's haircut, he looked in the mirror. He groaned. "This isn't cool at all," he said.

A few weeks later, Marcus saw Brian at the park. "Curly again?" he asked.

"Curly again," said Brian.

Clues	**Prior Knowledge**

Inference

Overview Making Inferences in Nonfiction

Directions and Sample Answers for Activity Pages

Day 1	See "Provide a Real-World Example" below.
Day 2	Read and discuss the passage. Then ask students to color the circles in front of the best answers. (**1:** People had many laws about horses. The book is about United States history. **2:** People make laws about things that are important to them. **3:** Horses were an important part of United States history.)
Day 3	Read and discuss the e-mail. Then ask students to complete the sentences. (**1:** ribbons with scissors, beads with small cups. **2:** ribbon/beads. **3:** fractions. **4:** fractions.)
Day 4	Read and discuss the passage. Then ask students to write their ideas in the boxes. (**Evidence:** The recipe does not include flour, sugar, baking powder, or salt. **Already Know:** Flour, sugar, baking powder, and salt are all dry ingredients. **Inference:** A cake mix includes all the dry ingredients needed for a cake.)
Day 5	Read the passage together. Ask students to record evidence, prior knowledge, and an inference. Afterward, meet individually with students to discuss their results. Use their responses to plan further instruction and review. (**Evidence:** Tickets go on sale on June 1. The ticket prices go up each day. **Prior Knowledge:** People like to save money on tickets. **Inference:** The circus will sell the most tickets on June 1.)

Provide a Real-World Example

◆ Hand out the Day 1 activity page.

◆ **Say:** *While driving home yesterday, I saw an ambulance coming toward me with its red lights flashing. Then I noticed some neighbors walking to their car, looking worried. What do you think happened?* Remind students that they can use evidence from the situation along with their own prior knowledge to figure out, or infer, what happened.

◆ Invite students to share their inferences. **Ask:** *What evidence did I give you? What prior knowledge did you use to help make the inference?* Remind them that an inference, while logical, may not always be correct.

◆ Ask students to study the evidence in the "Who Did It?" drawings on the page and use their prior knowledge to write an inference for each one. Allow time for students to share and compare their results.

◆ Explain that they can also make inferences when they read. Write the following on chart paper:

Making Inferences in Nonfiction

Find evidence in the pictures.

Find evidence in the passage.

Think about what you already know.

Try to figure out what the author does not state.

Who Did It?

Study each picture. Look for evidence. Then make an inference.

Inference

_____

_____

_____

_____

_____

Inference

_____

_____

_____

_____

_____

Curious Laws from Long Ago

Read the book review. Then read the questions and color the circles in front of the best answers.

Name of Book: *Curious Laws from Long Ago*

Author: Mary E. Simpson

Number of Pages: 180

Comments: This book was interesting. I learned a lot about United States history. I especially liked the unusual laws about horses. Here are some of them:

It is illegal to ride an ugly horse.

It is illegal to fish from horseback.

It is illegal to ride a horse up the stairs of the county court house.

It is illegal to open an umbrella on the street, for fear of it spooking horses.

All cars entering the city limits must first sound their horns to warn the horses of their arrival.

1. Which pieces of evidence are in the passage?

○ People had many different laws about horses.

○ People have few laws about horses today.

○ The book is about United States history.

2. What do you already know?

○ Fishing from horseback is dangerous.

○ People make laws about things that are important to them.

○ Many people worry about spooking horses when driving in cities today.

3. Which is the best inference?

○ All laws from long ago were unusual.

○ All these laws are still laws today.

○ Horses were an important part of United States history.

Math Review

Read the e-mail. Then complete each sentence.

Hey, Dad! I can't believe you're clear across the country. We miss you, but at least we can e-mail!

I've decided my favorite class is math. Ms. Ammaus makes it really fun. She brought in snack bags of cereal when we reviewed multiplication and division, and she used carrot sticks to show us some great tricks for remembering the nines. When we reviewed shapes and solids, she brought in little sandwiches, mini-pizzas, oranges, and drink boxes. (Luckily, math class isn't around lunch time!) It doesn't look like we'll be snacking tomorrow, though. I saw her bring in some ribbons with scissors and some beads with small cups. I'll e-mail again tomorrow night to tell you what our next review unit was!

Love,

Jamaica

1. Tomorrow Jamaica's class will use _____ and _____ for math.

2. I know you can cut a _____ into parts and divide a set of _____ into parts.

3. I know that parts of objects or parts of a set of objects are _____.

4. I can infer that Jamaica's class will review _____ tomorrow.

Baking a Cake

Read the passage. Then write your ideas in the boxes.

Have you ever baked a cake? Most cake recipes have the same basic ingredients. Some basic dry ingredients are flour, sugar, baking powder, and salt. Some basic wet ingredients are eggs, oil, and water or milk. The baker must measure each ingredient carefully so the cake will have the right texture and taste. However, some cakes require little measuring. Try this recipe:

> 1 box of yellow cake mix
> 1/4 cup vegetable oil
> 1/2 cup water
> 1 egg
> Mix ingredients well. Pour into a greased 8 x 8 inch pan. Bake at 350 degrees for 25 minutes. Cool and cut.

I know from the passage that . . .

I already know . . .

I can infer that . . .

Assessment

Read the advertisement. Then write the evidence, your prior knowledge, and an inference in the boxes.

Circus in town!
Come one, come all!

Saturday, June 7
County Fairgrounds
Tickets go on sale June 1.

Ticket Prices:
June 1: $5
June 2: $7
June 3: $9
June 4: $11
June 5: $13
June 6: $15
June 7: $17

Evidence

Prior Knowledge

Inference

Overview Drawing Conclusions in Fiction

Directions and Sample Answers for Activity Pages

Day 1	See "Provide a Real-World Example" below.
Day 2	Read and discuss the story. Then ask students to circle the clues and the best conclusion. (**Clues:** missed quite a few shots, something was wrong, breathing hard, missed five free throws, wasn't herself, stumbled a couple of times, couldn't tell she's the best player, sweating a lot. **Conclusion:** Amanda wasn't feeling well at the game last night.)
Day 3	Read and discuss the story. Then ask students to complete the sentences. (**1:** blinking digits. **2:** blinking digits. **3:** blinking digits. **4:** reset all the blinking clocks. **5:** The electricity went off and came back on during the night, disrupting the clocks.)
Day 4	Read and discuss the story. Then ask students to color the circles in front of the best answers. (**1:** Eagle would not invite Tortoise to his home. Eagle never said thank you. Eagle refused to make dinner for Tortoise. Tortoise made dinner for Eagle night after night. **2:** Eagle is selfish.)
Day 5	Read the story together. Ask students to write the story clues and a conclusion on their graphic organizers. Afterward, meet individually with students to discuss their results. Use their responses to plan further instruction and review. (**Clues:** The girls had a fun two weeks. Brenda shook Charlotte awake the day Dad and Mom were coming home. The girls mopped, washed dishes, washed the towels, collected the trash, dusted, and vacuumed the house before their parents got home. **Conclusion:** The girls didn't want their parents to know they hadn't kept the house clean.)

Provide a Real-World Example

◆ Hand out the Day 1 activity page.

◆ Write "Family Members," "Favorite Movie," and "After-School Activities" on cards. Make enough cards to have one for each student. Pass out the cards and ask students to fill in each category about themselves.

◆ Shuffle the cards. One at a time, invite students to choose a card and read the clues aloud. **Say:** *Using several clues to figure something out is drawing a conclusion. Use these clues to draw a conclusion about which classmate filled out this card.*

◆ After all the students have had a turn, ask them to record the information from their chosen card onto their sheets. **Say:** *The conclusion will be your classmate's name.*

◆ Explain that they can draw conclusions when they read stories. Write the following on chart paper:

Drawing Conclusions in Fiction

Find clues in pictures.

Find clues in the story.

Think about what makes sense based on the clues.

Who Is It?

Use clues to figure out which classmate is being described.

Family Members

+

Favorite Movie

+

After-School Activities

=

Conclusion

What Happened to Amanda?

Read the story. Then draw a circle around the clues and the best conclusion.

"I wonder what happened to Amanda last night?" asked Suni. "She's the best player on the team, but you couldn't tell it by the way she played."

"I know!" said Mariska. "She missed five free throws in a row. She stumbled a couple of times when she was dribbling. Everyone kept passing her the ball, but even when she was in a great position to score, she missed quite a few."

"We should give her a break," said Karin. "I know she's our captain, and we all missed her usual enthusiasm, but did you notice she was breathing hard and sweating a lot? Something was wrong."

"Let's give her a call," said Suni. "Even though she wasn't herself, she did help us win the game."

"Yes," said Mariska. "Let's tell her thanks for all she does for our team."

Clues

missed quite a few shots	wasn't herself
didn't dribble as much	broke the rules
something was wrong	stumbled a couple of times
passed the ball off to everyone else	missed the game
breathing hard	couldn't tell she's the best player
missed five free throws	sweating a lot

Conclusion

Amanda's teammates are angry with her.

Amanda doesn't enjoy playing basketball any more.

Amanda wasn't feeling well at the game last night.

Blink!

Read the story. Then complete each sentence.

"Yeah, it's Saturday!" Mario said with a yawn. He glanced at his alarm clock to see what time it was, but all he saw were digits going blink . . . blink . . . blink . . . "Hmm . . ." Mario thought.

Mario got dressed and wandered to the kitchen where Dad was reading the paper. "Good morning!" said Dad. "You can warm up some of those waffles in the microwave."

When Mario started to set the timer, he saw it again—blink . . . blink . . . blink . . . "Not again!" said Mario.

Dad looked up and laughed. Then he pointed to the clock on the oven—blinking! And the clock on the radio—blinking! And the clock in the hall—blinking!

"It's a good thing I have a watch," said Dad. "It's 8:36. Let's get busy and reset all these blinking clocks!"

1. When Mario looked at his alarm clock, he saw _____

_____.

2. When Mario tried to set the microwave timer, he saw _____

_____.

**3. When Mario looked at the oven clock, radio clock, and hall clock,
he saw** _____.

4. Dad said he and Mario needed to _____

_____.

5. I can conclude that _____

_____.

Tortoise and Eagle

Read the story. Then read the questions and color the circles in front of the best answers.

Tortoise saw Eagle flying overhead. "Come join me for dinner!" he called.

Eagle accepted the invitation, gobbled the delicious meal, and left without saying thank you. The next evening, he again flew over Tortoise's home, and Tortoise again invited him to eat.

The same thing happened night after night. Finally, Tortoise said, "Why don't you make dinner tomorrow night? I'd love to see your home!"

Eagle laughed mockingly. "I live in the sky. You'll never be able to come to MY home."

Tortoise was kind, but he was also clever. He offered Eagle a gourd full of leftovers to take home. However, instead of leftovers, Tortoise himself hid in the gourd. When Eagle got home, Tortoise crawled out and said, "My, what a lovely home! Is it time for dinner?"

"No!" Eagle shouted, throwing Tortoise into a lake. Sadly, Tortoise floated home. And he never invited Eagle to dinner again.

1. Which clues are in the story?

○ Eagle would not invite Tortoise to his home.

○ Eagle never said thank you.

○ Tortoise did not like being in Eagle's home.

○ Eagle refused to make dinner for Tortoise.

○ Tortoise made dinner for Eagle night after night.

○ Tortoise gave Eagle a gourd filled with food.

2. Which is the best conclusion?

○ Eagle is hungry.

○ Eagle is selfish.

○ Eagle is lonely.

Assessment

**Read the story. Then write the story clues
and a conclusion in the boxes.**

"Brenda, you're in charge of the house and
Charlotte while we're away," said Mom and
Dad. "When we get back, Dad will drive you
back to college."

Brenda and her younger sister had a fun two weeks. They ate what they liked,
watched movies, played games, and went for walks in the rain. Then, one morning,
Brenda shook Charlotte awake. "Dad and Mom will be home today! We'd better
get busy!"

Soon, Brenda was carrying a bucket of soapy water and a mop into the muddy
hall, while Charlotte washed the dirty dishes piled in the sink. Then, they threw
dirty towels into the washing machine and collected the pizza boxes, take-out
containers, and soda bottles around the house. Finally, they dusted, vacuumed,
and folded the towels. Just as the last towel was going into the cabinet, the garage
door opened.

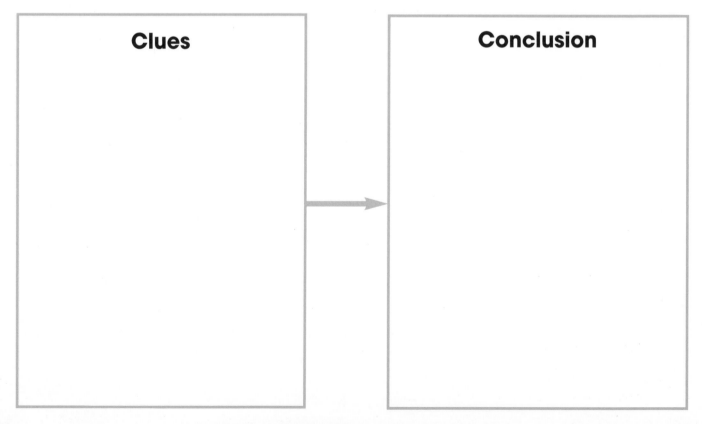

Clues	Conclusion

Overview Drawing Conclusions in Nonfiction

Directions and Sample Answers for Activity Pages

Day 1	See "Provide a Real-World Example" below.
Day 2	Read and discuss the passage. Then ask students to circle the evidence and best conclusion. (**Evidence:** tree stump has rings, grow well with plenty of water and sunshine, layers are on trunk, some are light-colored and wide, new layer of wood every year, rings are layers of wood, some are dark and narrow, drought and floods can interfere with growth. **Conclusion:** Scientists can study tree rings to learn about past weather conditions.)
Day 3	Read and discuss the passage. Then ask students to answer the questions. (**1:** They encountered cold, rain, snow, winds, hail, and sandstorms. **2:** They were sick and weak a great deal of the time. **3:** Many of the men endured injuries. **4:** The explorers faced buffalo, grizzly bears, wolves, and rattlesnakes. **5:** The Lewis and Clark expedition was dangerous.)
Day 4	Read and discuss the passage. Then ask students to color the circles in front of the best answers. (**1:** The potassium in bananas is good for people's hearts. The potassium in bananas can lower blood pressure and protect the stomach. Bananas are good for people's bones. Bananas give people energy. **2:** A banana is a healthy fruit.)
Day 5	Read the passage together. Ask students to write the evidence and a conclusion on their graphic organizers. Afterward, meet individually with students to discuss their results. Use their responses to plan further instruction and review. (**Evidence:** phobia, intense fear, skyscraper, top of a mountain, long bridge over a river, Ferris wheel, last row in a stadium, standing on a ladder. **Conclusion:** Fear of heights is one kind of phobia.)

Provide a Real-World Example

◆ Hand out the Day 1 activity page.

◆ **Say:** *I drove by an old house and noticed that a man was painting it. Another man was putting shingles on the roof. A woman was fixing a porch rail.* Remind students that using several clues to figure something out is drawing a conclusion. **Ask:** *What conclusion can you draw from this situation?*

◆ Invite students to share their conclusions. **Ask:** *What evidence did you use to draw your conclusion?*

◆ Ask students to study the evidence in the "Day at the Park" pictures on the page and write a conclusion for each set. Allow time for students to share and compare their results.

◆ Explain that they can also draw conclusions when they read. Write the following on chart paper:

Drawing Conclusions in Nonfiction

Find evidence in pictures.

Find evidence in the text.

Think about what makes sense based on the evidence.

Day at the Park

Study the pictures. Look for evidence. Then draw conclusions.

Conclusion

Conclusion

Tree Rings

Read the passage. Then draw a circle around the evidence and the best conclusion.

Every year, a tree adds a new layer of wood to its trunk. You can see these layers in a tree someone has cut down. The tree stump has rings inside it. Each ring is a layer of wood. If a ring is light-colored and wide, the tree got plenty of water, sunshine, and food that year. Weather conditions were good, and the tree grew well. If a ring is dark and narrow, something interfered with its growth. This is often a result of severe weather conditions, such as droughts or floods.

Evidence

tree stump has rings

grow well with plenty of water and sunshine

trees grow new stumps every year

layers are on trunk

some are light-colored and wide

some are dark and wide

new layer of wood every year

some are light-colored and narrow

people cut down trees in severe weather

rings are layers of wood

some are dark and narrow

droughts and floods can interfere with growth

Conclusion

Scientists can study weather conditions to learn about tree rings.
Scientists can study tree rings to learn about past weather conditions.
Tree rings are interesting to look at, but they are not important to scientists.

Lewis and Clark

Read the passage. Then answer each question.

President Thomas Jefferson decided to find out what the unexplored "far west" of America was like. He asked Meriwether Lewis and William Clark to lead an expedition. According to their journals, they encountered many kinds of harsh weather, such as cold, rain, snow, winds, hail, and sandstorms. Everyone on the expedition was sick and weak a great deal of the time. They suffered from fevers, boils, stomach distress, and disease. Many of the men endured injuries as a result of boating accidents and serious falls in the rugged mountains. Wild animals were a constant threat, too, as the explorers faced buffalo, grizzly bears, wolves, and rattlesnakes.

1. What kinds of weather did Lewis and Clark encounter on their journey?

_____

2. How did the men on the expedition feel during the journey?

_____

3. What else affected how the men felt?

_____

4. What wild animals did the men face?

_____

5. What can you conclude about the expedition?

_____

Banana Facts

Read the passage. Then read the questions and color the circles in front of the best answers.

   Bananas are a good source of potassium, a mineral important for nutrition. Studies show that potassium is good for people's hearts and can lower blood pressure. Researchers have learned that potassium-rich bananas also protect the stomach. Even bones seem to benefit from a diet that includes bananas. Many people who participate in sports or other forms of exercise eat bananas for energy. For example, a banana can replace some of the vitamins and minerals that bikers and runners lose as a result of their physical activity. A banana is easy to eat—no washing required. And it's soft, creamy, and sweet!

1. Which pieces of evidence are in the passage?

○ Researchers like to eat bananas.

○ The potassium in bananas is good for people's hearts.

○ The potassium in bananas can lower blood pressure and protect the stomach.

○ Bikers and runners like the taste of bananas.

○ Bananas are good for people's bones.

○ Bananas give people energy.

2. Which is the best conclusion?

○ A banana is a healthy fruit.

○ A banana is a sweet fruit that most people enjoy.

○ A banana is the best fruit choice because it's so easy to eat.

Assessment

Read the passage. Then write the evidence and a conclusion in the boxes.

A phobia is an intense fear of a particular thing or situation. For example, some people won't go to the top of a skyscraper because looking out the windows would terrify them. They won't climb to the top of a mountain, no matter how spectacular the view might be. They'll go miles out of their way to avoid driving across a long bridge over a river. They miss out on fun, such as riding a Ferris wheel or watching a sporting event from the last row of seats in a stadium. Even a simple everyday chore like changing a lightbulb panics them if it means standing on a ladder.

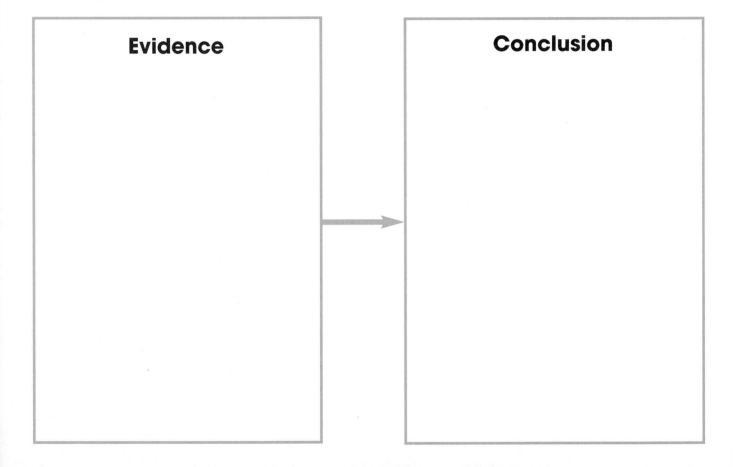

Evidence

Conclusion

Overview Evaluating Author's Purpose in Fiction

Directions and Sample Answers for Activity Pages

Day 1	See "Provide a Real-World Example" below.
Day 2	Read and discuss the story. Then ask students to color the circles in front of the best answers. (**1:** Max doesn't think the bag will work on him, but it does. The boys are at The Joke Store. A small yellow bag is laughing. Everyone in the store is roaring with laughter. **2:** to entertain readers with a story about laugh bags.)
Day 3	Read and discuss the story. Then ask students to complete the clues and write the author's purpose. (**1:** talk. **2:** talk. **3:** meeting. **4:** haughty. **5:** quarreled, fought. **6:** ducks, swans'. **Author's Purpose:** The author wants to entertain readers with a pourquoi tale that explains something in nature.)
Day 4	Read and discuss the story. Then ask students to answer the questions. (**1:** He played with bears and mountain lions. He was raised by coyotes. He used a rattlesnake for a whip. His ranch covered the whole state of New Mexico. **2:** The author wanted to entertain readers with a tall tale that has funny details and exaggeration.)
Day 5	Read the story together. Ask students to record clues and an author's purpose on their graphic organizers. Afterward, meet individually with students to discuss their results. Use their responses to plan further instruction and review. (**Clues:** rumor that the house is haunted, hears strange sounds in the night, hears footsteps on the stairs, hears tapping at her bedroom door, sees a pillow floating over the sofa, hears the doorbell ring but no one is there. **Author's Purpose:** The author wants to entertain readers with a ghost story.)

Provide a Real-World Example

◆ Hand out the Day 1 activity page.

◆ **Say:** *The title of this page is* Funny Pictures. *What is funny, unusual, or surprising about the first picture? Why do you think the artist drew this picture?*

◆ Allow time for students to discuss their ideas. Then ask them to write a caption for the picture and share it with the group. Repeat the process with the other pictures on the page.

◆ **Say:** *Artists often draw pictures to entertain. Authors often write to entertain, too. We can look for clues to help evaluate the author's purpose when we read.* Write the following on chart paper:

Evaluating Author's Purpose in Fiction

Find clues in the pictures.

Find clues in the story.

Think like the author.

Think about how the author tries to entertain.

Funny Pictures

Discuss why you think the artist drew these pictures. Then write a caption for each picture.

Caption:

_____

_____

Caption:

_____

_____

Caption:

_____

_____

Who's Laughing?

Read the story. Then read the questions and color the circles in front of the best answers.

"I've always wanted to come to The Joke Store," Bob said.

"Me, too!" said Charlie. "It must be pretty fun, because someone is sure laughing!"

The laughing didn't stop, and soon Bob and Charlie were laughing at the laughing. In fact, everyone in the store was roaring with laughter.

Soon, the boys noticed several people gathered in one aisle of the store. The clerk was holding a small yellow bag. Every time he squeezed it, it laughed for more than a minute. "So that's it! cried Bob. "I'm going to buy one of those!"

"Me, too! said Charlie.

The boys stopped by Bob's apartment first and told his brother Max what they'd bought. "It won't work on me," Max declared. But soon, Bob's whole family was in stitches.

"Let's go to my apartment now," said Charlie. "My family could use a good laugh, too!"

1. Which are clues about why the author wrote this story?

◯ Max doesn't think the bag will work on him, but it does.

◯ The boys are at The Joke Store.

◯ The boys want to buy something.

◯ A small yellow bag is laughing.

◯ A clerk works at the store.

◯ Everyone in the store is roaring with laughter.

2. Which is the author's main purpose?

◯ to inform readers about laugh bags

◯ to entertain readers with a story about laugh bags

◯ to persuade readers to buy a laugh bag

How Swans Got Long Necks

**Read the story. Look for funny, unusual, or surprising details.
Then complete the clues and write the author's purpose.**

Swans have always had beautiful feathers. They
have always been graceful swimmers. But they haven't
always had long necks. It all started in a duck pond
long ago.

"May we swim in your pond?" asked a flock of swans.

"Sure!" said the ducks. "The more the merrier."

Soon, the head swan called a meeting. "These ducks are not as lovely as we are.
They don't glide across the water as we do. Let's make them go away!" The other
swans, as haughty as their leader, agreed.

Soon, a big quarrel ensued, and then a fight. The ducks began to pull on the
swans' necks. When the fighting finally stopped, the swans' necks were several
inches longer. "We'll share," they mumbled, swimming to the other side of the
pond. But to this day, swans still have long necks.

Clues:

1. The swans can _____.

2. The ducks can _____.

3. The head swan called a _____.

4. The swans were _____.

5. The swans and ducks _____ and _____.

6. The _____ made the _____ necks several
   inches longer.

Author's Purpose: _____

_____

Pecos Bill

Read the story. Then answer the questions.

Pecos Bill was born on the plains of Texas. From the beginning, he was one tough cowboy!

"I wish Bill would quit playing with the bears and mountain lions," his mother complained when he was a baby.

One day, Bill was riding in a wagon with his parents. They never saw him fall out near the Pecos River.

"I miss Mom and Dad," said Bill. "But it's fun being raised by coyotes!" Soon, everyone began calling him Pecos Bill.

Pecos Bill worked as a cowhand, herding nasty bulls. He used a rattlesnake for a whip. Later, he had his own ranch. Was it big? Yep! It covered the whole state of New Mexico! Pecos Bill had to drain the Rio Grande to water his animals.

1. What did you read about . . .

Bill as a baby? _____

Bill growing up? _____

Pecos Bill's whip? _____

Pecos Bill's ranch? _____

2. Why do you think the author wrote this story?

_____

_____

Assessment

Read the story. Then write the clues and author's purpose in the boxes.

"Why do you want to live in that old house by yourself?" asked Lou's friend Bett. "You have no neighbors close by. And rumor has it that the house is haunted!"

Lou laughed. "I'm pretty sure those rumors are correct. I hear strange sounds in the night. I hear footsteps on the stairs, and sometimes I hear tapping at my bedroom door."

"Whoa—that would scare me to death!" said Bett.

"You haven't heard the best part yet," said Lou. "One night I saw a pillow floating over the sofa. Just as I was reaching for it, the doorbell rang. No one was there, and when I returned, the pillow was back in its place."

"Remind me not to visit you at night!" said Bett.

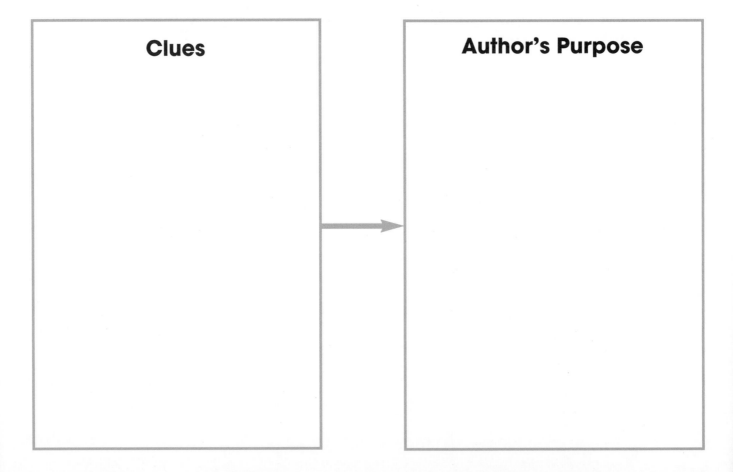

Clues	Author's Purpose

Overview Evaluating Author's Purpose in Nonfiction

Directions and Sample Answers for Activity Pages

Day 1	See "Provide a Real-World Example" below.
Day 2	Read and discuss the passage. Then ask students to color the circles in front of the best answers. (**1:** A tuba in a marching band is called a sousaphone. The tuba makes the lowest sound of all brass instruments. Some tubas have six valves. A tuba is the largest brass instrument. **2:** to inform readers about tubas.)
Day 3	Read and discuss the vacation brochure. Then ask students to answer the questions. (**1:** The author wants to persuade readers to come to Hawaii for a vacation. **2:** perfect, breathtaking, spectacular, amazing, fresh, sunny, dazzling, delicious, friendly, beautiful.)
Day 4	Read and discuss the passage. Then ask students to draw a picture to go with the passage and write the author's purpose. (**Drawing:** Responses will vary but may include a family having a banquet, a decorated room, an open window, oranges, flowers, red envelopes and dollar bills, Chinese lanterns hanging in a street, or a child carrying a lantern in a parade. **Author's Purpose:** The author wants to inform readers about Chinese New Year.)
Day 5	Read the advertisement together. Ask students to record evidence and an author's purpose on their graphic organizers. Afterward, meet individually with students to discuss their results. Use their responses to plan further instruction and review. (**Evidence:** make kids look cool, fabulous patterns, name printed at no extra charge, grade-A quality, comfortable, help kids be more organized, great prices, going fast. **Author's Purpose:** The author wants to persuade readers to buy a Sporty Pack.)

Provide a Real-World Example

◆ Hand out the Day 1 activity page.

◆ **Say:** *My aunt asked me to go to a movie. I wasn't sure I wanted to see it. She said a reviewer gave it five stars, and two friends raved about it. Why do you think my aunt said these things? What was she trying to do?*

◆ Discuss the things your aunt said to try to persuade you to go to the movie. Then ask students to complete the sentences by the movie picture.

◆ Ask students to look at the next picture, determine what the girl wants, and write two things she might say to her dad to persuade him to see things her way. Allow time for students to share their responses.

◆ **Say:** *Sometimes authors write nonfiction to persuade. Other times, they write nonfiction to inform. We can look for evidence to help evaluate the author's purpose when we read.* Write the following on chart paper:

Evaluating Author's Purpose in Nonfiction

Find evidence in the pictures.

Find evidence in the text.

Think like the author.

Think about how the author tries to persuade or inform.

Please?

Listen to the example. Then complete the sentences.

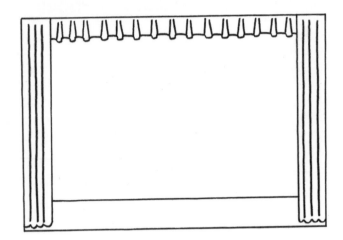

A _____ gave the movie _____.

Two friends _____ **about the movie.**

Write two things this girl might say to her dad.

1. _____

   _____

2. _____

   _____

OOM-PAH-PAH!

**Read the passage. Then read the questions
and color the circles in front of the best answers.**

Have you ever listened to a band or orchestra? The musicians' instruments are divided into different categories, including strings, percussion, woodwinds, and brass. The largest brass instrument is the tuba. A tuba is made of about sixteen feet of tubing and can have from three to six valves to change the instrument's pitch. An orchestra has only one tuba player. Tubas in concert bands are smaller, while tubas in marching bands, called sousaphones, are bigger. A tuba rests on a seated musician's lap in an upright position, but a sousaphone wraps around the player and rests on his or her left shoulder. The tuba makes the lowest sound of all brass instruments. One familiar sound is *OOM-PAH-PAH!*

1. Which sentences are evidence that help you figure out the author's purpose?

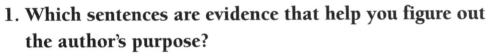

○ A tuba in a marching band is called a sousaphone.

○ OOM-PAH-PAH is a funny tuba sound.

○ The tuba makes the lowest sound of all brass instruments.

○ Some tubas have six valves.

○ A tuba is the largest brass instrument.

○ Many kids want to play the tuba in the school band.

2. Which is the author's main purpose?

○ to entertain readers with a story about a tuba player

○ to persuade readers to learn to play a tuba

○ to inform readers about tubas

Vacation Destination

Read the travel brochure. Then answer each question.

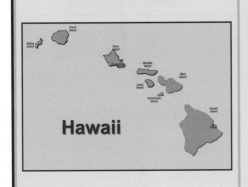

Come Visit Hawaii!

Hawaii

Hawaii is the perfect destination for your next vacation! Each of its six major islands offers the traveler a breathtaking experience. The turquoise ocean, towering sea cliffs, thundering surf, spectacular canyons, and active volcanoes are only a few of the amazing sights. The air is fresh, the days are sunny, and the flowers are dazzling. Vacationers can enjoy a delicious Hawaiian feast called a luau. Every luau includes entertainment, often traditional hula dancing. The friendly people of Hawaii are always ready to welcome visitors to their beautiful island state!

1. What is the author's main purpose in writing this travel brochure?

_____

2. What are six of the adjectives the author uses to support this purpose?

_____

_____

_____

_____

Chinese New Year

Read the passage. Draw a picture to go with the passage. Then write the author's purpose.

Chinese New Year occurs on a different date each year, but it is usually in January or February. In China, the traditional New Year celebrations last for fifteen days and end with a full moon. Everyone spends New Year's Eve at home where family members gather to honor ancestors with a banquet. On New Year's Day, families decorate their houses. They open their windows to let the old year out. They buy oranges and flowers, especially plum and peach blossoms. They also put dollar bills in red envelopes to give away. On the last day of Chinese New Year, people hang lanterns in the streets for the Lantern Festival. That night, children carry homemade lanterns in a parade.

Author's Purpose:

_____

_____

Assessment

Read the advertisement. Then write the evidence and author's purpose in the boxes.

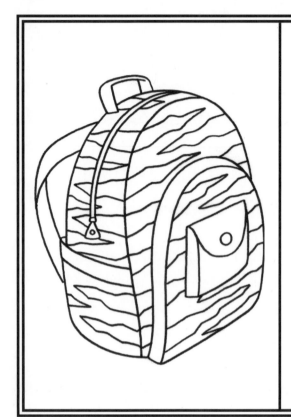

Need a backpack for school?
Want to look cool?
Then get a Sporty Pack today!

• Choose one of our fabulous patterns, like leopard spots or tiger stripes.

• Get your name printed at no extra charge!

• Our packs are Grade-A quality. Super-comfortable padded straps! Strong, dependable zippers!

• Outside and inside pockets—you'll be the most organized kid in school!

Buy now! Great prices!
Sporty Packs are going fast!

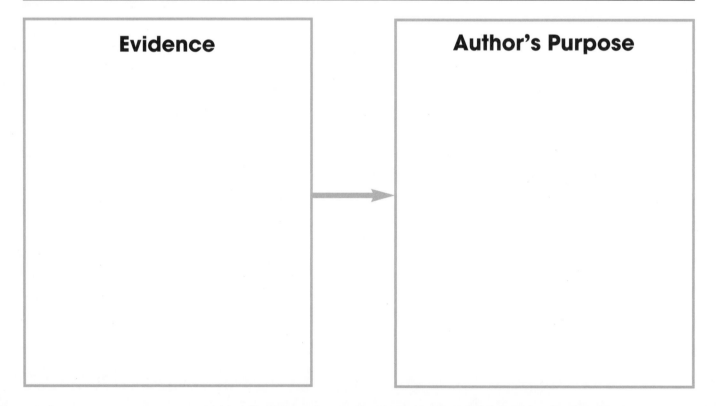

Evidence

Author's Purpose

Overview Analyzing Text Structure and Organization in Fiction

Directions and Sample Answers for Activity Pages

Day 1	See "Provide a Real-World Example" below.
Day 2	Read and discuss the story. Then ask students to circle the three main text structures the author uses. (description, sequence of events, compare and contrast)
Day 3	Read and discuss the story. Then ask students to follow the directions and complete the sentences. (**1:** sequence of events. **2:** problem and solution, the speaker system quits working.)
Day 4	Read and discuss the story. Then ask students to complete the sentences. (**1:** he made all 10,000 lakes in Minnesota. **2:** winters were so cold in the lumber camp. **3:** he sank right into the ground. **4:** cause and effect.)
Day 5	Read the story together. Ask students to record clues about the main text structure on their graphic organizers. Afterward, meet individually with students to discuss their results. Use their responses to plan further instruction and review. (**Clues:** author uses sequence signal words to tell the steps Clara and Tia use to make the mask—**first, after that, then, next, final,** and **last. Text Structure:** sequence of events.)

Provide a Real-World Example

◆ Hand out the Day 1 activity page.

◆ **Say:** *A friend just got home from a ski trip. He told me what he saw. He told me what he heard. He told me how the falling snow felt on his face. He even told me how the food in the lodge smelled and tasted. From these clues, I could tell my friend was describing his ski trip.*

◆ Ask students to read the description of the ski slope on their page. Then ask them to draw a picture based on the description. Allow time for students to compare drawings with their classmates.

◆ **Say:** *Description is one type of text structure we find when we read stories. We also find four other text structures.* Write the following on chart paper:

Analyzing Text Structure and Organization in Fiction

Look for
- **words that describe**
- **words that compare and contrast**
- **words that tell about cause and effect**
- **words that tell about a sequence of events**
- **words that tell about a problem and a solution**

Ski Slope

Read the story. Then draw a picture based on the descriptions you read.

Nick looked at the ski slope. At the top, one skier was waving and shouting. Another skier had just reached the bottom. Cool snowflakes tickled Nick's face. Suddenly, he smelled spicy pizza. He decided to have a slice before getting on the chair lift.

City Mouse and Country Mouse

Read the story. Think about the clues. Then draw a circle around the three main text structures the author uses.

"Hi, Cousin!" said Country Mouse to City Mouse. "Welcome to the farm! We're having my favorite dinner—crunchy sunflower seeds, shiny dandelion greens, and chewy bread crusts."

City Mouse didn't like this country food at all. "Say, why don't you come back to the city with me? We'll have one of MY favorite meals!" he said.

Country Mouse followed his cousin back to the city. First, they had sugary frosting from a leftover chunk of chocolate cake. Then they had creamy bits of cheese that had fallen off someone's sandwich. They even had real applesauce from a container they found in a trash can. "Yum!" said Country Mouse.

Even though the food was good, Country Mouse liked his country food better than city food. He couldn't enjoy eating the city food. Cars honked. Music blared. People yelled. "Thank you," he said. "But I must go back home now. Maybe you can visit again next year!"

"I will, if you'll visit me!" said City Mouse with a smile.

Text Structures:

Description

Sequence of Events

Compare and Contrast

Cause and Effect

Problem and Solution

Costume Parade

Read the story. Then follow the directions and complete the sentences.

Tina looked around. Lovely ladies, creepy monsters, and cartoon characters all waited for the principal's announcement from the speaker on the wall. She smoothed her scarecrow costume and adjusted her hat impatiently.

Suddenly, the secretary came into the room. "The speaker system quit working. Please line up in the hall for instructions," she requested.

As they left the classroom, Tina's teacher put on a mask and became the big, bad wolf. After everyone was in line, the principal started the costume parade. First, the kindergarten children followed her. Then, the other grades followed in order. Finally, everyone was outside, marching around the school.

Tina saw her mom and several neighbors waiting along the sidewalk. "Hi, it's me—Tina!" she called, smiling and waving. Soon, the parade was over and everyone returned to their classrooms. But before they got back to work, the speaker crackled. "Thanks for the great parade!" their principal said.

1. Draw a line under each of these words: **as, after, first, then, finally, soon,** and

   before. These are signal words for the _____

   text structure.

2. The author also uses the _____ text structure to show

   what the principal does when _____.

Paul Bunyan

Read the story. Then complete the sentences.

Have you ever heard of Paul Bunyan? He was one big lumberjack! Did you know he made all 10,000 lakes in Minnesota? He did! And all because he was stomping around cutting down trees. (He leaves HUGE footprints, you know!) Paul loved his animals, too. One was Lucy the Purple Cow. Since winters were so cold in the lumber camp, Lucy's milk turned to ice cream right in the bucket. And we can't forget Babe the Blue Ox. He was enormous! Once a blacksmith tried to carry some metal shoes he'd made for Babe and sank right into the ground!

1. **Paul stomped around with his big feet while cutting down trees in Minnesota. As a result,** _____

   _____.

2. **Lucy the Purple Cow's milk turned to ice cream right in the bucket, because** _____

   _____.

3. **A blacksmith tried to carry Babe the Blue Ox's heavy metal shoes. Consequently,** _____

   _____.

4. **Based on these clues, the text structure for this story is**

   _____.

Assessment

**Read the story. Then write clues about the
main text structure on the graphic organizer.**

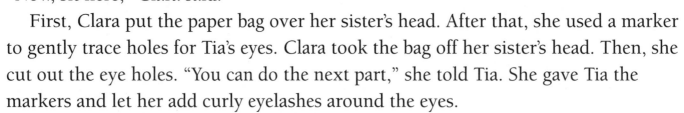

"Let's make an elephant mask," Clara said to her
little sister Tia. "You can help. Please get two paper bags,
a scissors, some markers, and glue."

Tia raced around the house to collect the items.
"Now, sit here," Clara said.

First, Clara put the paper bag over her sister's head. After that, she used a marker
to gently trace holes for Tia's eyes. Clara took the bag off her sister's head. Then, she
cut out the eye holes. "You can do the next part," she told Tia. She gave Tia the
markers and let her add curly eyelashes around the eyes.

"Now we're ready for the final steps," said Clara. She cut out a trunk and
two large ears from the second paper bag. Last of all, she glued the trunk and ears
on to the mask.

"There you go, Tia!" Clara said.

"Thanks, Clara!" said Tia. "Can we make a tiger mask now?"

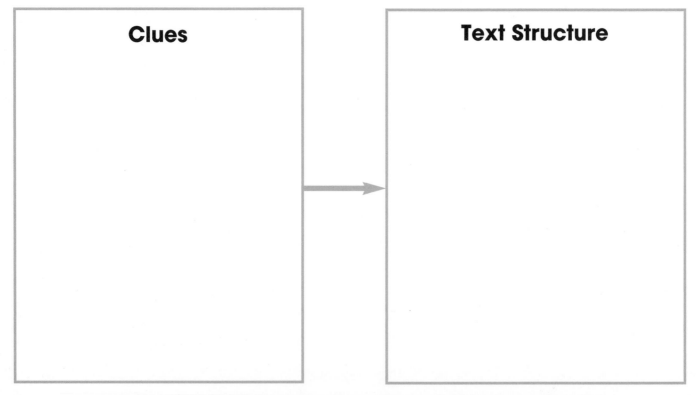

Clues

Text Structure

Overview Analyzing Text Structure and Organization in Nonfiction

Directions and Sample Answers for Activity Pages

Day 1	See "Provide a Real-World Example" below.
Day 2	Read and discuss the passage. Then ask students to circle the two main text structures the author uses. (description, compare and contrast)
Day 3	Read and discuss the passage. Then ask students to follow the directions and complete the sentences. (**1:** cause and effect. **2:** sequence of events, make pearls.)
Day 4	Read and discuss the passage. Then ask students to complete the sentences. (**1:** went to South Africa to work for a law firm. **2:** that the British leaders treated Indian people unfairly. **3:** stayed in South Africa to help the Indian people. **4:** returned to India to help the people there. **5:** a sequence of events.)
Day 5	Read and discuss the passage. Ask students to record information about the main text structure on their graphic organizers. Afterward, meet individually with students to discuss their results. Use their responses to plan further instruction and review. (**Evidence:** saw the suffering of animals in America, went to England to learn about the RSPCA, founded the ASPCA, helped pass laws against cruelty to animals, spoke about animal rights. **Text Structure:** problem and solution.)

Provide a Real-World Example

◆ Hand out the Day 1 activity page.

◆ **Say:** *I recently read directions for making a pasta necklace. First, you get pasta of different shapes and colors. Then, you dip a toothpick in water and use it to make holes in the pasta pieces. Next, you let the pasta dry. Finally, you string the pasta pieces on yarn with a needle. From this evidence, I knew the text structure was a sequence of events. In a how-to text, we also call this text structure* **steps in a process**.

◆ Ask students to number the pictures on the page to show the correct order. Then ask them to read the passage and draw sketches to show the sequence of events. Allow time for students to share their drawings.

◆ **Say:** *Sequence of events is one type of text structure we find when we read. We also find four other text structures.* Write the following on chart paper:

Analyzing Text Structure and Organization in Nonfiction

Look for
- **words that describe**
- **words that compare and contrast**
- **words that tell about cause and effect**
- **words that tell about a sequence of events**
- **words that tell about a problem and a solution**

Name _____

Things to Make

Listen to the example. Then number the pictures to show the correct order.

Read the passage. Then draw the sequence of events in the boxes.

I couldn't decide what to make for the school science fair. First, I went to the library and browsed some science books. Then, I talked to my uncle who works in a lab. Next, I looked at a Web site with photos of other kids' projects. Finally, I decided to design a new type of recycling container. That way, my family can use my project at home after the science fair is over.

Sharks

Read the passage. Think about the evidence. Then draw a circle around the two main text structures the author uses.

Two types of sharks are the tiger shark and great white shark. Each is over fifteen feet long and weighs over 2,200 pounds. The two sharks also have similar teeth—sharp and triangular with serrated edges. The great white shark has a gray back, while a young tiger shark has dark stripes on its back. The sharks have an extraordinary sense of smell in common, which helps them hunt. Unlike the tiger shark, a great white shark can go without food for a month after an especially large meal. Another way the great white shark is different is that it must move twenty-four hours a day in order to get oxygen into its bloodstream. Unfortunately, both sharks are alike in one disastrous way— they both attack humans.

Text Structures:

Description

Sequence of Events

Compare and Contrast

Cause and Effect

Problem and Solution

Pearls

Read the passage. Then follow the directions and complete the sentences.

    People use pearls to make beautiful jewelry. Clams and mussels form some pearls, but most are formed by oysters. As an oyster grows, its shell grows with it. The part of the oyster that produces its shell is called the mantle. Sometimes a small object, such as a grain of sand, gets between the oyster's shell and the mantle. Because this object feels irritating, the oyster covers it with a material called nacre. The layers of nacre build up, resulting in a pearl. A pearl that forms naturally like this rarely has a perfectly round shape. However, if people insert round, shiny beads between the shell and mantle, the oysters form round, shiny pearls that are called cultured pearls. Cultured pearls aren't as rare as round and shiny natural pearls. Therefore, they cost less.

1. Draw a line under the words **because, resulting in, if,** and **therefore**. These are signal words for the _____ text structure.

2. The author also uses the _____ text structure to show how oysters _____.

A Nonviolent Leader

Read the passage. Then complete the sentences.

Mohandas Gandhi was a great leader. He was born in India in 1869. As an adult, he went to England, where he studied to become a lawyer. Then he went to South Africa to work for a law firm. South Africa was ruled by the British, and Gandhi soon discovered that they treated the Indian people who lived there unfairly. After Gandhi's job ended, he stayed in South Africa to help the Indian people. He led their struggle without using violence. Finally, twenty years later, he went back to India. After he returned home, Gandhi led another nonviolent struggle for the Indian people. It ended on August 15, 1947, when India gained its freedom from British rule.

1. After Gandhi studied law in England, he _____

_____.

2. Soon after this, Gandhi discovered _____

_____.

3. Gandhi's job ended. Then, he _____

_____.

4. After twenty years, Gandhi _____

_____.

5. Based on these clues, the text structure for this story is _____

_____.

Assessment

Read the passage. Then write evidence about the main text structure on the graphic organizer.

   In the 1800s in England, people mistreated many working animals. In 1835, concerned people founded the Royal Society for the Prevention of Cruelty to Animals (RSPCA). In America, Henry Bergh saw the suffering of animals, too. People forced dogs to pull heavy carts. People whipped horses that didn't pull streetcars fast enough. People drowned stray animals. Bergh went to England to learn about the RSPCA. When he returned, he founded the American Society for the Prevention of Cruelty to Animals (ASPCA). He also encouraged the state government in New York to pass laws against cruelty to animals. Then, Bergh traveled throughout America to speak about animal rights. By 1873, twenty-five states and territories had formed animal protection groups.

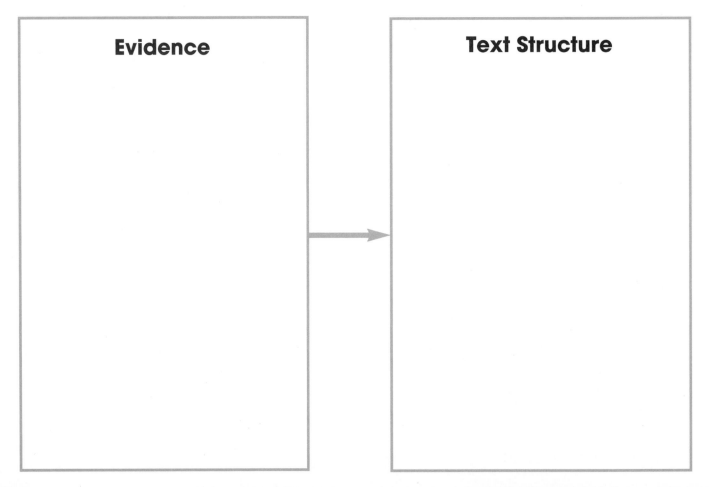

Evidence

Text Structure

Overview Using Text Features to Locate Information

Directions and Sample Answers for Activity Pages

Day 1	See "Provide a Real-World Example" below.
Day 2	Read and discuss the page. Then ask students to answer the questions. (**1:** The Life Cycle of Bees. **2:** Carol Pugliano-Martin. **3:** page 2. **4:** page 10. **5:** Chapter 1. **6:** Answers will vary. **7:** Introduction and/or Summary. **8:** Answers will vary.)
Day 3	Read and discuss the page. Then ask students to color the circles in front of the best answers. (**1:** Rachel Carson. **2:** Historical Perspective. **3:** to point to the photo that goes with the caption. **4:** college. **5:** Rachel learned to use many tools in the college lab. **6:** Rachel Carson's Nature Books.)
Day 4	Read and discuss the page. Then ask students to complete the sentences. (**1:** alphabetical. **2:** alphabetical. **3:** numbers that can be divided by two, such as 2, 4, and 6. **4:** pattern. **5:** 10. **6:** area patterns and number patterns. **7:** checkerboard pattern, quilts. **8:** how to find or make patterns. **9:** Answers will vary.)
Day 5	Provide each student with a nonfiction book that includes a title page, table of contents, chapter headings, captions, sidebars, a glossary, and an index. Ask students to use the book to complete the chart. Afterward, meet individually with students to discuss their results. Use their responses to plan further instruction and review. (Answers will vary.)

Provide a Real-World Example

◆ Select a nonfiction book with a title page, table of contents, chapter headings, captions, sidebars, a glossary, and an index. Provide each student with a nonfiction book.

◆ Hand out the Day 1 activity page.

◆ **Say:** *Nonfiction books have certain text features. We use these text features to locate, or find, information in the book.*

◆ Hold up your book. **Say:** *First, I will look at the title page. The title page shows the title and author of the book.* Point to the title and author's name as you read them aloud.

◆ **Say:** *Look at your book. Does your book have a title page? Read the title and author's name to a partner. Then put a check mark in the* title page *box on your chart.*

◆ Repeat the process for the remaining text features, first pointing one out in your book and then asking students to see if it is included in their books.
Ask: *What does each text feature tell us?* Discuss their findings.

◆ **Say:** *This week we will learn more about these text features.* Write the following on chart paper:

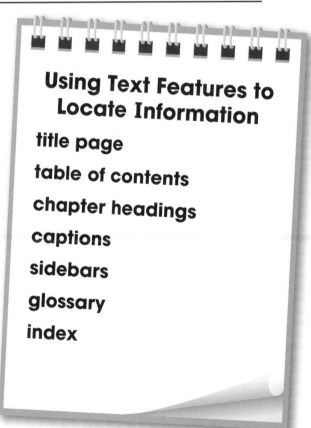

Using Text Features to Locate Information

title page

table of contents

chapter headings

captions

sidebars

glossary

index

Front to Back

Select a nonfiction book. Check off each text feature your book includes. Then explain the purpose of each feature.

✔	text feature	What does this feature tell us?
	title page	
	table of contents	
	chapter headings	
	captions	
	sidebars	
	glossary	
	index	

Starting Out

Previewing the title page, table of contents, and chapter headings helps you get ready to read a book. In this book, the table of contents is on the title page. Read the page. Then answer the questions.

1. What is the title of the book?

   _____

2. Who is the author?

   _____

3. On what page will you begin reading the book? _____

4. What page would you go to if you want to learn about types of bees? _____

5. Which chapter might tell about bee eggs? _____

6. What is one thing you might read about in Chapter 3? _____

   _____

7. Where would you find information about the whole book?_____

8. What might be another good title for this book?

   _____

Captions and Sidebars

A caption tells more information about a picture.
A sidebar tells more information about a topic.
Read the following caption and sidebar from
a book called *Rachel Carson: The Beauty of Nature*.
Then read the questions and color the circles
in front of the best answers.

A Young Writer

Rachel loved more than nature. She also loved to write. At age eleven, she had her first story published in a magazine for young writers. She decided to study writing in school.

Her love of nature never left her, though. Rachel decided she wanted to be a scientist, too. She studied biology, worked in a lab, and did research. Over time, she combined her two interests into one job. She became one of the most famous nature writers ever.

Historical Perspective

Today women do many kinds of work. When Carson was born, not many women went to college. Very few women became scientists.

As a college student, ▶ Rachel Carson became interested in science.

1. **Who is this page about?**
   - ○ Rachel Carson
   - ○ college students

2. **What is the sidebar heading?**
   - ○ A Young Writer
   - ○ Historical Perspective

3. **Why does the page have an arrow?**
   - ○ to point to the photo that goes with the caption
   - ○ to point to the photo that goes with the sidebar

4. **Which key word is in both the sidebar and the caption?**
   - ○ work
   - ○ college

5. **Which would be another good caption for the photo?**
   - ○ Rachel wrote many nature books.
   - ○ Rachel learned to use many tools in the college lab.

6. **Which would be another good sidebar topic for this page?**
   - ○ Hobbies for Eleven-Year-Olds
   - ○ Rachel Carson's Nature Books

Glossary and Index

A glossary defines key words in a book.
The index shows where to find words.
In this book, the glossary and index
are on the same page. Read the page.
Then complete the sentences.

•••••••••••• Glossary ••••••••••••

area patterns (AIR-ee-uh PAT-ernz): A pattern that repeats
   up and down and across

even numbers (EEV-en NUM-berz): Numbers that can be
   divided by two, such as 2, 4, or 6

number patterns (NUM-ber PAT-ernz): Numbers arranged so
   that the values of the numbers form a pattern

odd numbers (AHD NUM-berz): Numbers that cannot be
   divided by two, such as 3, 5, or 7

pattern (PAT-ern): Something that repeats over and over

•••••••••••• Index ••••••••••••

area patterns 9, 10, 11,
checkerboard pattern 10
number patterns 11, 12, 13
quilts 17

20

1. The words in the glossary are in _____ order.

2. The words in the index are in _____ order.

3. Even numbers are _____.

4. Something that repeats over and over is a _____.

5. You can learn about the checkerboard pattern on page _____.

6. On page 11, you can read about _____.

7. Two entries in the index that are not defined in the glossary are

   _____.

8. This book is probably about _____.

9. A good title for this book might be _____

   _____.

Assessment

Use your book to complete the chart.

	Page Number	**One Thing I Learned**
title page		
table of contents		
chapter heading		
caption		
sidebar		
glossary		
index		

Overview Using Graphic Features to Interpret Information

Directions and Sample Answers for Activity Pages

Day 1	See "Provide a Real-World Example" below.
Day 2	Discuss the time line and map. Then ask students to complete the sentences. (**Timeline:** 1200–1400; 1532; Inca Empire; Manco Capac; 1200. **Map:** South America; Peru, Cuzco; east; Andes Mountains.)
Day 3	Read and discuss the table and chart. Then ask students to answer the questions. (**Table:** Lake Huron; Lake Michigan; Lake Erie and Lake Michigan; Lake Superior; Lake Huron and Lake Michigan. The information stays the same. **Chart:** Indiana; Milwaukee; Detroit; Illinois; Cleveland. The information in the Population column can change.)
Day 4	Discuss the graphs. Then ask students to circle the facts they learn from each graph. (**Pie Graph:** Most of the animals were dogs. People bring birds and cats to the SPCA. Dogs and cats make up nearly 75% of the animals. **Bar Graph:** more than 5,500 nesting pairs in 1998; fewer than 1,200 nesting pairs in 1981; over 1,000 more nesting pairs in 1994 than in 1991.)
Day 5	Provide each student with a nonfiction book that includes at least three of the graphic features on the list. Ask students to use the book to complete the chart. Afterward, meet individually with students to discuss their results. Use their responses to plan further instruction and review. (Answers will vary.)

Provide a Real-World Example

◆ Select a nonfiction book that has photographs, illustrations, and labeled diagrams. Provide each student with a nonfiction book.

◆ **Say:** *Nonfiction texts have graphic features. Readers must know how to interpret, or figure out, the information on a graphic feature. Pictures are one important type of graphic feature. Pictures can be photographs, illustrations, or labeled diagrams.*

◆ Share some photographs, illustrations, and labeled diagrams from your book. Discuss why the author used each one and what readers can learn from them. Then invite students to look through their own books and find photographs, illustrations, and labeled diagrams to share with the group.

◆ Hand out the Day 1 activity page. Discuss the pictures. Then ask students to color the circle in front of the reason the author used each one. (**1:** The book is about famous inventors. **2:** It shows a time long ago when people didn't have cameras. **3:** It shows parts we could not see in a photograph.)

◆ **Say:** *This week we will learn about some other graphic features, too.* Write the following on chart paper:

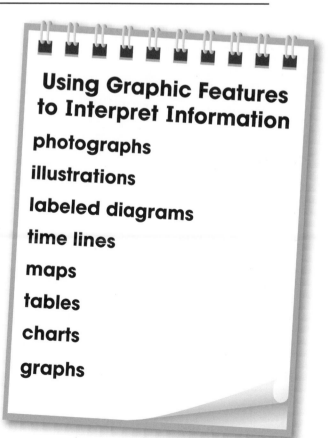

Using Graphic Features to Interpret Information

photographs

illustrations

labeled diagrams

time lines

maps

tables

charts

graphs

Pictures

1. Why do you think the author used this photograph?

○ The book is about famous musicians.

○ The book is about famous inventors.

○ The book is about famous teachers.

2. Why do you think the author used this illustration instead of a photograph?

○ It shows something people imagined.

○ It shows parts we could not see in a photograph.

○ It shows a time long ago when people didn't have cameras.

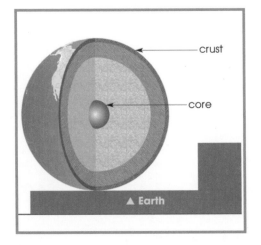

3. Why do you think the author used this labeled diagram instead of a photograph?

○ It shows parts we could not see in a photograph.

○ It shows where the United States is on Earth.

○ It tells how hot Earth's core is.

Time lines and Maps

A time line tells when things happen. A map shows where things happen. This time line and map are from a book called *The Inca World*. Complete the sentences about each graphic feature.

Time Line

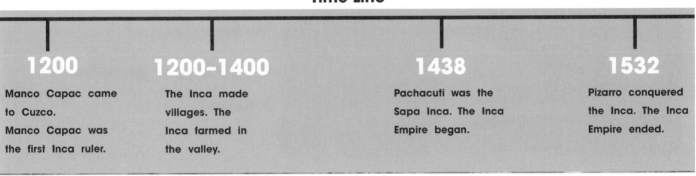

1200	1200–1400	1438	1532
Manco Capac came to Cuzco. Manco Capac was the first Inca ruler.	The Inca made villages. The Inca farmed in the valley.	Pachacuti was the Sapa Inca. The Inca Empire began.	Pizarro conquered the Inca. The Inca Empire ended.

The Inca made villages in the years _____.

Pizarro conquered the Inca in the year _____. In 1438, the

_____ began. The first ruler in Cuzco was

_____. He came to Cuzco in the year _____.

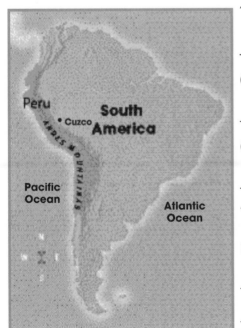

This is a map of a continent. The continent is

_____.

One country in this continent is

_____.

One city in the country is

_____.

The arrows show the directions on

the map. The Atlantic Ocean is on the

_____ side of the continent. The

_____ are on the west coast.

Tables and Charts

A table shows information that stays the same in each column. A chart shows information that can change in one or more columns. This table and chart are from a book called *The Midwest Region.* Answer the questions about each graphic feature.

Lake	States	Size
Lake Erie	Michigan, Ohio, New York, Pennsylvania	10,000 square miles (26,000 square kilometers)
Lake Huron	Michigan	23,000 square miles (59,500 square kilometers)
Lake Michigan	Illinois, Indiana, Michigan, Wisconsin	22,300 square miles (57,750 square kilometers)
Lake Superior	Michigan, Minnesota, Wisconsin	32,000 square miles (82,800 square kilometers)

Which lake is only in Michigan? _____

Which lake is partly in Indiana? _____

Which lakes are in four different states?_____

Which lake is largest? _____

Which lakes are similar in size? _____

Why is this a table instead of a chart?

_____

City	State	Population
Chicago	Illinois	2,896,000
Cleveland	Ohio	478,403
Detroit	Michigan	900,198
Indianapolis	Indiana	791,926
Milwaukee	Wisconsin	583,624

What state is Indianapolis in?

_____

What is a city in Wisconsin? _____

Which city has a little over 900,000 people? _____

Which state has a city with over two million people? _____

Which city is smallest? _____

Why is this a chart instead of a table?

_____

Graphs

A graph is a way to show how information is related. Look at the pie graph and bar graph. Draw a circle around the facts you learn from each graph.

Animal Protection Percentages

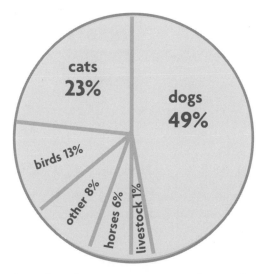

The Society for the Prevention of Cruelty to Animals (SPCA) in Houston took in 508 animals in one month.

- Most of the animals were dogs.
- The smallest percentage of animals were horses.
- People bring birds and cats to the SPCA.
- People bring more livestock than birds to the SPCA.
- Dogs and cats make up nearly 75% of the animals.

Nesting Pairs of Bald Eagles in the Lower Forty-Eight States

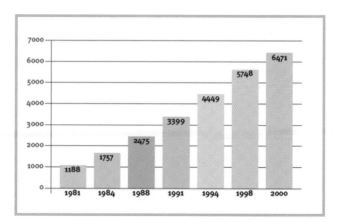

The bald eagle was once listed as an endangered animal in the United States. After that, researchers counted more every year.

Researchers counted . . .
- more than 5,500 pairs in 1998
- more than twice as many nesting pairs in 1988 than in 1984
- the largest gain between 1998 and 2000
- fewer than 1,200 nesting pairs in 1981
- more than 1,000 more nesting pairs in 1994 than in 1991

Name _____

Assessment

**Look at the list of graphic features. Choose three that you find in your book.
Then complete the chart.**

Graphic Features		
photograph illustration labeled diagram	time line map	table chart graph

Graphic Feature	Description	One Thing I Learned

   Unit 26 • *Everyday Comprehension Intervention Activities Grade 4* • ©2010 Newmark Learning, LLC

Overview Distinguishing and Evaluating Fact and Opinion I

Directions and Sample Answers for Activity Pages

Day 1	See "Provide a Real-World Example" below.
Day 2	Read and discuss the passage. Then ask students to write **fact** or **opinion** after each statement. (**1:** opinion. **2:** fact. **3:** opinion. **4:** fact. **5:** fact. **6:** opinion.)
Day 3	Read and discuss the passage. Then ask students to write each sentence in the correct box. (**Facts:** 2, 3, 6. **Opinions:** 1, 4, 5.)
Day 4	Read and discuss the passage. Then ask students to circle **fact** or **opinion** for the statements. (**1:** opinion. **2:** fact. **3:** fact. **4:** opinion. **5:** fact. **6:** opinion.)
Day 5	Read the passage together. Ask students to record the facts, opinions, and evidence on their graphic organizers. Afterward, meet individually with students to discuss their results. Use their responses to plan further instruction and review. (**Facts:** in many amusement parks; invented by George Washington Gale Ferris, Jr; designed for 1893 World's Fair in Chicago; 250 feet tall; weighed 2,200 tons; 36 cars; 40 passengers in each car; took apart; put back together; 1904 World's Fair in St. Louis; destroyed in 1906. **How I Know:** The author can prove these statements true through research. **Opinions:** today's aren't as exciting; one of the most impressive structures ever built; should have been placed in a museum. **How I Know:** The author can't prove these statements true. Some people might disagree with them. The author uses words such as **exciting**, **impressive**, and **should**.)

Provide a Real-World Example

◆ Hand out the Day 1 activity page.

◆ **Say:** *San Francisco is a city in California. San Francisco is a beautiful city. The first statement is a fact. I can prove this fact. No one can disagree with it. The second statement is an opinion. I personally believe this statement, and I can give reasons to back up my belief, but some people might disagree with me.*

◆ Discuss ways you can prove facts. Encourage students to find San Francisco on a map. Then discuss the word **beautiful**. **Say:** *Opinions include descriptive words such as **pretty**, **ugly**, **nice**, **mean**, **best**, or **worst**, and belief words such as **should** or **shouldn't** that some people agree with and others do not.*

◆ Allow time for students to record the fact and opinion about California on their page. Then repeat the process for the statements *Ice cream is a frozen dessert. Ice cream is bad for you.*

◆ Explain that students can also distinguish and evaluate fact and opinion when they read. Write the following on chart paper:

Distinguishing and Evaluating Fact and Opinion

A statement you can prove true is a fact.

You can prove a fact by personal observation or by relying on experts.

A statement you cannot prove true is an opinion.

An opinion includes words that tell or describe what someone believes.

Can You Prove It?

Listen to each example. Then complete each fact or opinion.

Fact: San Francisco is a _____ in _____.

Opinion: San Francisco is a _____ city.

Fact: Ice cream is a _____ dessert.

Opinion: Ice cream is _____ for you.

The Siberian Tiger

Read the passage. Then write _fact_ or _opinion_ after each statement.

The Siberian tiger is a handsome animal. It's also
the biggest cat on Earth! It eats more than twenty
pounds of meat each day, mostly deer and wild pigs.
The Siberian tiger looks vicious with its large,
strong body and sharp claws and teeth. Because of
Siberia's cold climate, the tiger has a long, thick
coat. The female tiger gives birth to three or four
cubs, who stay with their mother for three to five
years. During this time, the tiger teaches the cubs
to hunt. She is a good mother.

1. **The Siberian tiger is a handsome animal.**   _____

2. **The Siberian tiger eats deer and wild pigs.**   _____

3. **The Siberian tiger looks vicious**.   _____

4. **A female Siberian tiger gives birth to
   three or four cubs.**   _____

5. **Siberian tiger cubs stay with their mother
   for three to five years.**   _____

6. **A female Siberian tiger is a good mother.**   _____

Bowling

Read the passage. Then write each sentence in the correct box.

Bowling is an easy sport to learn. A machine sets up ten pins at the end of a sixty-foot alley. The players, called bowlers, each choose a ball. Bowling balls come in terrific colors and can weigh up to 16 pounds. The first bowler rolls the ball down the alley, trying to knock down all ten pins. If all the pins fall, the bowler gets a strike. If not, the bowler gets another try. Then, the next bowler takes a turn. A game of bowling consists of ten frames. The bowler who has knocked down the most pins at the end of the game is the winner. Everyone should try bowling—it's fun!

1. **Bowling balls come in terrific colors.**
2. **A bowling alley is sixty feet long.**
3. **A bowling ball can weigh sixteen pounds.**
4. **Bowling is an easy sport to learn.**
5. **Everyone should try bowling.**
6. **A strike occurs when a bowler knocks down all ten pins in one roll.**

Facts	Opinions

Bicycles Are the Best

**Read the passage. Then circle *fact* or *opinion*
for each statement.**

   Bicycles are the best means of transportation.
Unlike motor vehicles, bicycles don't pollute
the air. Many towns and cities have bicycle paths.
Riding on a bicycle path is safer than riding on
streets with traffic. Whether riding on a path or on the street, however, most bikers
wear bicycle helmets for protection. Because gasoline costs so much today, some
people are now riding bikes to work. This is a great idea for all working people.
Not only is bike riding fun, it's good for you, too. Studies show that regular biking
improves people's breathing, muscles, and mood.

1. **The best means of transportation is a bicycle.**   fact   opinion

2. **Bicycles don't pollute the air.**   fact   opinion

3. **Most bikers wear bicycle helmets on**   fact   opinion
   bike paths and streets.

4. **Bike riding is fun.**   fact   opinion

5. **Biking improves people's breathing.**   fact   opinion

6. **All working people should ride bikes to work.**   fact   opinion

Assessment

**Read the passage. Write the facts and how you know they're facts.
Then write the opinions and how you know they're opinions.**

Many amusement parks have Ferris wheels.
However, today's Ferris wheels aren't as exciting as the
old-fashioned kind. George Washington Gale Ferris, Jr,
invented the first Ferris wheel, and it was one of the most
impressive structures ever built. He designed the ride for
the 1893 World's Fair in Chicago. The wheel was 250 feet
tall and weighed 2,200 tons. It had 36 cars, and 40
passengers could ride in each car. When the fair ended,
workers took the Ferris wheel apart. A company bought it and put it back together
again. Then, the company took it to the 1904 World's Fair in St. Louis. In 1906, the
Ferris wheel was destroyed, but it should have been placed in a museum.

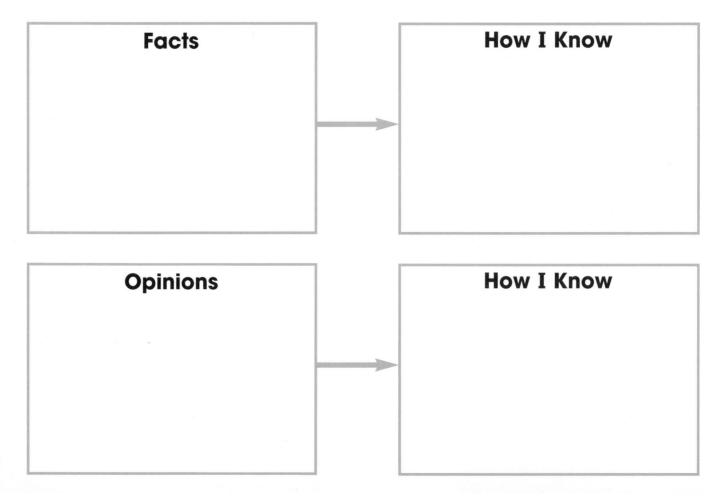

Facts	How I Know

Opinions	How I Know

Overview Distinguishing and Evaluating Fact and Opinion II

Directions and Sample Answers for Activity Pages

Day 1	See "Provide a Real-World Example" below.
Day 2	Read and discuss the passage. Then ask students to write facts and opinions about Yellowstone and to circle signal words. (**Facts:** Answers will vary. All statements that are not opinions are facts. **Opinions:** Yellowstone National Park is a wondrous place. Geysers are the best part of Yellowstone. Old Faithful is an amazing sight. **Signal Words: wondrous, best, amazing.**)
Day 3	Read and discuss the passage. Then ask students to write each sentence in the correct box. (**Facts:** 1, 4, 6. **Opinions:** 2, 3, 5.)
Day 4	Read and discuss the passage. Then ask students to circle **fact** or **opinion** for the statements. (**1:** fact. **2:** opinion. **3:** fact. **4:** opinion. **5:** opinion. **6:** fact.)
Day 5	Read the passage together. Ask students to record the facts, opinions, and evidence on their graphic organizers. Afterward, meet individually with students to discuss their results. Use their responses to plan further instruction and review. (**Facts:** filled with air, burner heats air, balloon rises, flows with the wind, pilots have received special training and a license, ride in a wicker basket, stand for the entire trip. **How I Know:** The author can prove these statements true through personal observation or research. **Opinions:** great fun, peaceful experience, not scary. **How I Know:** The author can't prove these statements true. Some people might disagree with them. The author uses words such as **great**, **peaceful**, and **not scary**.)

Provide a Real-World Example

◆ Hand out the Day 1 activity page.

◆ **Say:** *This page has facts and opinions about grizzly bears. You can prove a fact through personal observation or by relying on experts. No one can disagree with a fact. An opinion is something that someone personally believes. People can give reasons to back up their opinions, but other people might disagree with them. Opinions include descriptive words such as **easy** or **hard**, and belief words such as **should** or **shouldn't**.*

◆ Ask students to work with a partner to label each statement as a fact or opinion. (fact, opinion, fact, opinion) Encourage them to circle words that signal an opinion. Then, invite the partnerships to share and defend their answers for the group.

◆ Repeat the process for the statements about pizzas. (opinion, opinion, fact, fact)

◆ Remind students that they can also distinguish and evaluate fact and opinion when they read a passage. Review the chart created in the previous unit. Write the following on chart paper:

Distinguishing and Evaluating Fact and Opinion

A statement you can prove true is a fact.

You can prove a fact by personal observation or by relying on experts.

A statement you cannot prove true is an opinion.

An opinion includes words that tell or describe what someone believes.

How Do You Know?

Label each statement as a fact or an opinion.

A grizzly bear can weigh as much as 500 pounds.   _____

The grizzly bear is a magnificent animal.   _____

Grizzly bears live in Alaska.   _____

The mountains of Alaska are an amazing sight.   _____

Pizza makes a good meal.   _____

The worst kind of pizza is pineapple pizza.   _____

Pizza often has tomato sauce on it.   _____

Pizza was not created in Italy.   _____

The First National Park

Read the passage. Then follow the directions.

Yellowstone National Park is a wondrous place. It was America's first national park. Parts of Yellowstone are in three states: Wyoming, Montana, and Idaho. Visitors come to the park to hike, camp, fish, ride bikes, ride horses, and row boats. Visitors also come to observe the hundreds of geysers and hot springs throughout the park. The geysers are the best part of Yellowstone. Nearly everyone stops to see the geyser called Old Faithful. Every 35 to 120 minutes, its boiling water shoots as high as 180 feet. It's an amazing sight!

Write three facts about Yellowstone National Park.

1. _____.

2. _____.

3. _____.

**Write three opinions about Yellowstone National Park.
Then circle the descriptive words that signal an opinion.**

1. _____.

2. _____.

3. _____.

What's a Dogface?

Read the passage. Then write each sentence in the correct box.

Butterflying is an activity similar to birdwatching. People look for butterflies, identify them, and keep track of the different ones they see. Butterflies have intriguing names, such as Question Mark, Pepper and Salt, and Dogface. The Question Mark is an orange butterfly. The Pepper and Salt is dark brown with a few pale spots, and the Dogface is yellow. Some butterflies are tiny. For example, the Eastern Tail Blue measures only one-half inch. The Blue Morpho, on the other hand, has a wingspan of six inches. The Blue Morpho is a dazzling butterfly with shimmering blue wings. A day spent watching butterflies is a good day!

1. **The Dogface butterfly is yellow.**
2. **A day spent watching butterflies is a good day.**
3. **Butterflies have intriguing names.**
4. **The Eastern Tail Blue measures one-half inch.**
5. **The Blue Morpho is a dazzling butterfly.**
6. **Some people identify butterflies and keep track of the different ones they see.**

Facts	Opinions

Big Bird

Read the passage. Then circle *fact* or *opinion* for each statement.

What a strange bird the ostrich is! It is the largest bird in the world. Some male ostriches are nine feet tall! This big bird has long, strong legs and a long, sharp claw on each foot. The ostrich uses its legs and feet as weapons to fight off predators. An ostrich is peculiar in another way, too. Although it has feathers, it cannot fly! A male ostrich is a handsome bird with black and white feathers. The female's feathers are light brown. Female ostriches lay giant eggs that weigh about three pounds each. Ostriches live in Africa and eat plants, insects, and lizards.

1. A male ostrich can be nine feet tall.   fact   opinion

2. The ostrich is a strange bird.   fact   opinion

3. An ostrich egg weighs about three pounds.   fact   opinion

4. A bird that can't fly is peculiar.   fact   opinion

5. The male ostrich is a handsome bird.   fact   opinion

6. An ostrich uses its legs and feet to fight off predators.   fact   opinion

Assessment

**Read the passage. Write the facts and how you know they're
facts. Then write the opinions and how you know they're opinions.**

Have you ever seen a hot air balloon? This giant balloon
is filled with air. A burner heats the air by burning propane
gas. The heated air causes the balloon to rise. After floating
upward, the balloon flows along with the wind. Pilots who
fly hot air balloons have received special training and a
license. The pilot and passengers ride in a wicker basket
attached to the balloon. They stand for the entire trip.
Riding in a hot air balloon is great fun! Drifting through the
air is a peaceful experience. Even though the balloon goes
quite high, the ride is not scary.

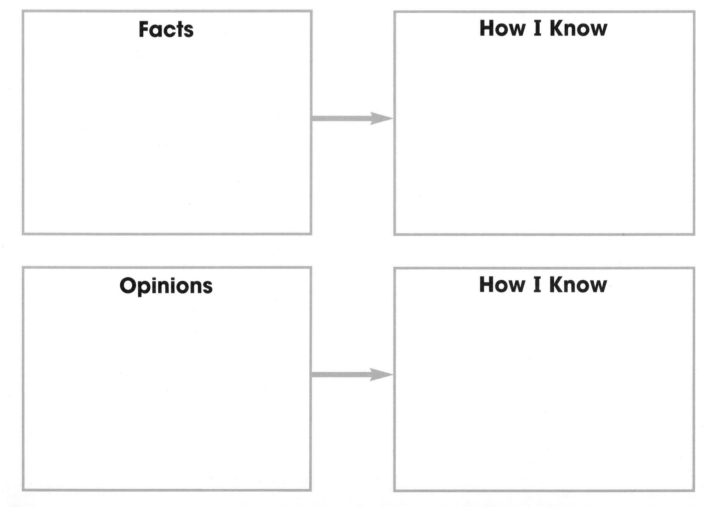

Facts	How I Know

Opinions	How I Know

Overview Making Judgments I

Directions and Sample Answers for Activity Pages

Day 1	See "Provide a Real-World Example" below.
Day 2	Read and discuss the passage. Then ask students to complete the sentences. (**Author's Judgment:** healthy snacks and drinks. **Evidence:** healthy machines, healthy snacks, soft drinks, healthy choices.)
Day 3	Read and discuss the passage. Then ask students to circle the best word choice for each sentence. (**1:** race. **2:** shortens. **3:** Greyhound rescue groups. **4:** less exercise **5:** good. **6:** does not approve.)
Day 4	Read and discuss the passage. Then ask students to color the circles in front of the best answers. (**1:** Skateboarding can be fun if you use the right board and safety gear. **2:** Getting hurt isn't fun. Dressing for safety is smart. Skateboarding pros wear safety gear. Skateboarding is dangerous.)
Day 5	Read the passage together. Ask students to record the evidence and author's judgment on their graphic organizers. Afterward, meet individually with students to discuss their results. Use their responses to plan further instruction and review. (**Evidence:** Can you imagine having a turkey on the Great Seal of the United States? Or on U.S. money and stamps? It's good that Congress didn't agree with Benjamin Franklin when choosing the national bird. **Author's Judgment:** The American bald eagle was the best choice for the U.S. national bird.)

Provide a Real-World Example

◆ Hand out the Day 1 activity page.

◆ **Say:** *When I was your age, my class had homework. Different parents had different ideas about homework. My friend Sue had to do her homework before she could play. What are some reasons her parents might have had that rule?* Allow time for students to discuss and record their ideas in the first column of the chart.

◆ **Say:** *My friend Ray got to play for an hour before he did his homework. His parents MADE him play! What are some reasons his parents might have had that rule?* Allow time for students to discuss and record their ideas in the second column of the chart.

◆ **Say:** *My parents and I talked about both rules and the evidence for each rule. My parents used the evidence to make a judgment. They felt that the evidence for the second rule was strongest. After that, I took a break before doing my homework.* Then explain that authors sometimes make judgments, too. Write the following on chart paper:

Making Judgments

Look for two sides of an issue.

Look at the evidence for both sides.

Look for words that show the author has chosen one side over the other.

Decide if you agree with the author's decision.

Homework Rules

Listen to the examples. Then write reasons for each rule.

Reasons to do homework before you play	Reasons to take a break before doing homework

Judgment:

_____

_____

Healthy Choices

Read the passage. Then complete the sentences.

Many schools have vending machines that earn money for the school. Often, these machines have unhealthy snacks and drinks, such as candy, cookies, chips, and sodas. Vending companies say these items sell the best. However, research indicates that schools sell just as much with "healthy machines."

Schools could improve the health of students, teachers, and staff members by providing only healthy choices in their vending machines. Those against changing the machines say healthier items like fresh fruit and vegetables would spoil. Rather than these choices, the machines could offer snacks such as wheat crackers, nuts, raisins, and dried cranberries. Milk, water, and 100% fruit juices could replace unhealthy soft drinks.

Author's Judgment:

Schools should have vending machines with _____.

Evidence Supporting Author's Judgment:

Schools can make just as much money with _____.

Wheat crackers, nuts, raisins, and dried cranberries are _____.

Milk, water, and 100% fruit juices are healthier than _____.

Students, teachers, and staff members would benefit from having _____

_____.

Greyhound Racing

**Read the passage. Then draw a circle around
the best word choice for each sentence.**

Many people are fans of greyhound racing.
They say that greyhounds love to run, and racing
gives them healthy, muscular bodies. But some
people feel greyhound racing is a cruel sport.
They are concerned that the dogs spend their whole
lives either on a racetrack or in a crate or pen. Then,
when their racing days are over when they are about
four years old, many are killed.

Greyhound rescue groups take unwanted racing dogs and try to find homes
for them. While waiting for adoption, the greyhounds live in kennels. Volunteers
wash and groom them, and the dogs get mild exercise every day. With its calm,
quiet—even polite—nature, this breed of dog makes a loving companion.
Greyhounds adopted into homes often live thirteen years.

1. **Some people feel that greyhounds love to (race, live in crates).**

2. **Other people feel that greyhound racing (lengthens, shortens)
   the dogs' lives.**

3. **(Greyhound racers, Greyhound rescue groups) try to find homes
   for unwanted racing dogs.**

4. **Kennels require (more exercise, less exercise) from greyhounds
   than racetracks require.**

5. **Greyhounds are (good, poor) companions for the people who adopt them.**

6. **From the evidence, it appears that the author (approves, does not approve)
   of greyhound racing.**

A Dangerous Sport

Read the passage. Then read the questions and color the circles in front of the best answers.

Skateboarding is a popular sport. It's fun, but it's also dangerous. Before trying skateboarding, make sure you have what you need. First, consider the board. Get the right skateboard for your age and size. You've borrowed a board and had no problems, you say? Maybe you had beginner's luck—but don't trust luck when it comes to your gear. Smart skateboarders dress for safety, including a helmet, elbow pads, wrist guards, knee pads, and shoes that won't slip. You don't think safety gear looks cool? Then look at the pros! It's true you'll be able to skate in your neighborhood or at some skate parks without protective gear. But injuries won't make skateboarding much fun!

1. What is the author's judgment about skateboarding?

  ⭘ Skateboarding is fun, so go ahead and try it.

  ⭘ Skateboarding can be fun if you use the right board and safety gear.

  ⭘ People should not skateboard, because it's too dangerous.

2. What pieces of evidence support the author's judgment?

  ⭘ Getting hurt isn't fun.

  ⭘ Borrowing a skateboard is okay sometimes.

  ⭘ Dressing for safety is smart.

  ⭘ Skateboarding gear doesn't look cool.

  ⭘ Skateboarding pros wear safety gear.

  ⭘ Skateboarding is dangerous.

Assessment

Read the passage. Then write the evidence and author's judgment in the boxes.

In 1782, the United States Congress chose the American bald eagle as the national bird. The members of Congress wanted a bird unique to the United States. They felt that the large, powerful eagle symbolized strength, courage, and freedom. However, some people thought this bird was a poor choice. For example, Benjamin Franklin believed that the bald eagle was a lazy bird and a coward. He thought that the turkey had more courage and was a truer native of America. Can you imagine having a turkey on the Great Seal of the United States? Or on U.S. money and stamps? Benjamin Franklin was a great man, but it's good that Congress didn't agree with him when choosing the national bird.

Evidence	Author's Judgment

Overview Making Judgments II

Directions and Sample Answers for Activity Pages

Day 1	See "Provide a Real-World Example" below.
Day 2	Read and discuss the editorial. Then ask students to circle the author's judgment, underline the evidence, and complete the sentence. (**Author's Judgment:** We must put these worries aside and begin offering our assistance. **Evidence:** The world will be a better place if we all stop to help one another. If you help people, they'll likely help others, creating a chain reaction. Somewhere along the line, you might be the one who benefits from that help. **Sentence:** Answers will vary.)
Day 3	Read and discuss the letter. Then ask students to circle the author's judgment and answer the questions. (**Author's Judgment:** We need to have school uniforms for Canwood Intermediate School. **1:** less peer pressure to deal with, fewer discipline problems, feel more like a team, focus more on learning, parents can save money. **2:** choosing own clothing is a protected right and an important way to express individuality. **3:** Answers will vary. **4:** Answers will vary.)
Day 4	Read and discuss the passage. Then ask students to color the circles in front of the best answers. (**1.** Wearing a bike helmet should be a law in all states for all ages. **2.** Bike helmets significantly lower the risk of brain injury. **3.** Some people say a helmet is too uncomfortable.)
Day 5	Read the passage together. Ask students to record the evidence and author's judgment on their graphic organizers. Afterward, meet individually with students to discuss their results. Use their responses to plan further instruction and review. (**Evidence:** The work gets done faster. Parents get more free time. Kids get the money they need. Kids learn valuable skills that will help them when they're old enough to get a real job someday. **Author's Judgment:** Getting paid for chores is a good idea.)

Provide a Real-World Example

◆ Hand out the Day 1 activity page.

◆ **Say:** *When I go to the grocery store, the clerk asks me if I want paper bags or plastic bags. Some people choose paper bags. They feel that using plastic bags is bad for the environment. What are some ways that using plastic bags is bad for the environment?* Allow time for students to discuss and record their ideas in the first column of the chart.

◆ **Say:** *Other people choose plastic bags. These people feel that using paper bags is bad for the environment. What are some ways that using paper bags is bad for the environment?* Allow time for students to discuss and record their ideas in the second column of the chart.

◆ **Say:** *Think about the evidence. Write your judgment on the line. Then share your judgment with a partner, including the evidence that supports your judgment.*

◆ Remind students that authors sometimes make judgments, too. Review the chart created in the previous unit. Write the following on chart paper:

Making Judgments

Look for two sides of an issue.

Look at the evidence for both sides.

Look for words that show the author has chosen one side over the other.

Decide if you agree with the author's decision.

Paper or Plastic?

Listen to each argument. Then use the chart to help make your judgment.

Problems with plastic bags	Problems with paper bags

My Judgment:

_____

_____

_____

Helping

Read the editorial. Draw a circle around the author's judgment.
Then underline the evidence that supports the author's judgment.

Editorial

Many people look the other way when they see someone in trouble. Perhaps the person is trying to open a heavy door while carrying several bags. Perhaps the person is in tears after a bad day. Perhaps a bully is making fun of the person.

I understand why people don't stop to help. They think they don't have time. They think it's none of their business. They think they might end up in trouble themselves. However, we must put these worries aside and begin offering our assistance. The world will be a better place if we all stop to help one another. If you help people, they'll likely help others, creating a chain reaction. And, who knows— somewhere along the line, YOU might be the one who benefits from that help!

Complete this sentence.

I (**agree, do not agree**) with the author's judgment, because

_____

_____

_____.

Letter to the Principal

Read the letter. Draw a circle around the author's judgment. Then answer the questions.

Dear Ms. March,

Yesterday a girl in my class was ridiculed because her parents can't afford to buy her a popular type of T-shirt. This happens to other kids, too— including me. To stop this problem, we need to have school uniforms for Canwood Intermediate School.

Some students would not like uniforms at first. These students feel that choosing their own clothing is a protected right and an important way to express their individuality. However, studies show that students who wear uniforms have less peer pressure to deal with and fewer discipline problems. The students feel more like a team and focus more on learning. In addition, parents can save money by buying, selling, and trading outgrown uniforms with other school families.

Thank you for considering my proposal.

Sincerely,

Jeb Walesh

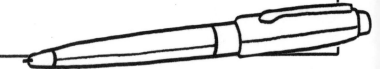

1. What evidence does Jeb give for wearing uniforms?

_____

2. What evidence does Jeb give for not wearing uniforms?

_____

3. Do you think Ms. March will agree with Jeb's judgment? Why or why not?

_____

4. Do you agree with Jeb's judgment? Why or why not?

_____

Bike Helmets

Read the passage. Then read the questions and color the circles in front of the best answers.

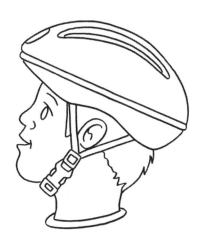

   Some states and communities have laws about wearing bike helmets. For example, the law may declare that anyone under age sixteen must wear a helmet when riding a bike. Other states and communities leave this decision up to the rider.

   People have different excuses for not wearing a helmet. Some people say a helmet is too expensive, too hot, or too uncomfortable. Others say they don't have time to take it on and off, or they forget to wear it. However, wearing a bike helmet should be a law in all states for all ages. Bike helmets protect riders in case of a fall. They significantly lower the risk of brain injury and even death. Isn't that worth more than an excuse? Wear a helmet!

1. What judgment does the author make?
○ More communities should have laws about wearing bike helmets.
○ Wearing a bike helmet should be a law in all states for all ages.
○ People should make bike helmets that are more comfortable.

2. What is one piece of evidence the author uses for making this judgment?
○ Bike helmets significantly lower the risk of brain injury.
○ People have different excuses for not wearing a helmet.
○ The law may declare that anyone under age sixteen must wear a helmet when riding a bike.

3. Why do some people disagree with the author's judgment?
○ Bike helmets protect riders in case of a fall.
○ Some states and communities leave the decision up to the rider.
○ Some people say a helmet is too uncomfortable.

Assessment

**Read the passage. Then write the evidence
and author's judgment in the boxes.**

Kids need money for different things. Sometimes they need cash for a field trip. Sometimes they need to buy a gift for a birthday party. Sometimes they want to go to a movie with a friend.

Some kids get an allowance to pay for these things. They don't have to do anything to get the money—their parents just give it to them. That works well in some families, but other parents disagree with this idea. These parents require their children to do certain chores in order to get paid. For example, kids might wash dishes, fold laundry, rake leaves, babysit younger brothers and sisters, or clean the garage.

Getting paid for chores is a good idea. Everyone pitches in, so the work gets done faster. Parents get more free time, and kids get the money they need. Plus, kids learn valuable skills that will help them when they're old enough to get a real job someday.

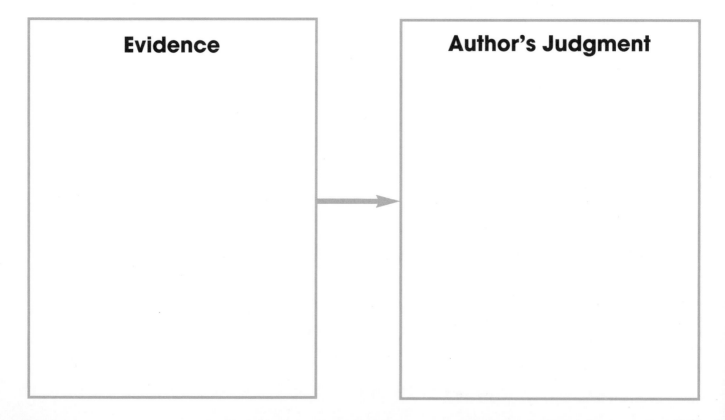

Evidence	**Author's Judgment**

Notes

Notes

Notes

Notes

Notes

Notes